If Angels were your Priests...

The Memoirs of Canon Stanislaus Condon (Father Stan) 1935-2012

Acknowledgments

For the Diocese of Northampton with special thanks to Shirley Hawes and Brian Plunkett without whose help and enthusiasm this book would not have been possible.

Maria – Louise Newitt

My grateful thanks to Jonathan Mortimer of Junior London for his invaluable help in designing and formatting this book.

Brian Plunkett

Preface

This is a very lively memoir although it confines itself to the life of a Catholic priest who took orders more than 50 years ago, when life and the church were far stricter than they are today. His life as an ordinary curate and priest at parishes in the East Midlands is told with a human and disarmingly humorous touch. In truth no parish priest is ordinary, nor is his life, one of celibacy and obedience to a spiritual hierarchy that fewer people the common room. It sounds like good training for narrowness of vision and an inability to empathise with the worries of future parishioners but the author sees its merits. Students of philosophy and theology, of all things, were not allowed to ask questions! The Hierarchy even among students was absolute – you progressed from tonsuring to being made a Dean. If this rigidity persists it could help to explain the falling off of vocations. With no previous practice at hearing confessions or leading Mass the author set out into the world at Corby, the new steel-making town in Northamptonshire. As junior curate and dogs body, to the priest in charge, he was expected to spend his free evenings sitting with him in silent contemplation of the television until bedtime. Father Ted it was not!

From there onwards the author charts his progress to full priesthood, changing homes, parishes, housekeepers and Bishops at regular intervals. He writes in a relaxed and amused tone so that one believes his parishioners, with all their peculiar problems, must have counted themselves lucky to have him. As the drastic reforms of the Vatican Council proceeded, bewildering the older member of the flock, congregations began their steady decline. He observes objectively: "People's need of and use of the Church was far greater than it is now". Loss of enthusiasm and observance in the family and the spread of ignorance of even basic Christianity, especially in Catholic schools, brings out his most trenchant opinions. He suggests it would had been better to close many Catholic secondary schools altogether rather than dilute them with so many indifferent pupils that they almost become an irreligious influence on the once - faithful. Like parents, like offspring. But when, after 45 years service, he reaches retirement, he reflects how lucky and happy has been a life which many of us would regard as one of pretty strenuous self-sacrifice. He barely hints at the fact that England is not his native land. I would liked to hear more of his origins (in wartime Poland) and how he comes to England. The acceptance he won in mainly rural English parishes as a pillar of the community is all the more to his credit. As a non – Catholic reader I was surprised at how closely involved I became in the story he tells so modestly but well. To an outsider the life of a Catholic Priest looks lonely and forbidding but – if you are made of the right stuff – it obviously can become humanly very rewarding. Many other devout Catholics would feel better for reading it.

Peter Lewis.

Introduction

It is surely wrong to maintain that an autobiography is just a glorified ego-trip in print or that it should be the prerogative of the famous, notorious, rich or influential. Every life is unique and special.

My Parent on their wedding day 1923

It is now accepted that autobiographies are written - either by the subjects themselves of by 'ghost writers' - by even very young men and women who, through their fame or notoriety, skill in sport or drama or politics or even crime, have met other famous people or affected, in one way or another, the lives of others. However, there are some lives which do not fall into any of these categories. These are lives which simply have a background which, through no merit of the individual, no effort or virtue on his part, are very different from the comparative norm; a sort of life which starts very far away, in all senses, from where it is now. There is no obvious connection between the start and the present and the journey in between may well be full of surprises and providential interventions.

It is just this lack of an obvious link between my present life as a parish priest and venerable Canon in Woburn Sands (now retired!) and my origin in Poland that prompted this bursting into print - and the occasional updating - and the possibility that anyone reading this may gain some insight into recent history and acknowledge the inscrutable wisdom and providence of God.

Father Stan

The purpose of a biography - ordinary or 'auto' - is not just to immortalise the person at its centre. Perhaps not even that at all. It gives an opportunity to set down a period of time and historical circumstances in a concrete, personalised manner rather than just theoretical and disembodied. It is to give a glimpse into a period, in this case, when children were allowed to rush out of class to look with wonder at a Zeppelin as it passed overhead.

When a person lives to be 92, all but a month or so, that life covers a tremendous stretch of change. When she - in this case, our mother - was born and reared in what the serious historians call 'the cockpit of Europe' then a biography of her casts light on a way of life, set of values and everyday circumstances completely different to anything known in a Britain which has not experienced occupation, loss of national identity or any such radical change since 1066!

A bit of a history lesson will not come amiss What is now known as Poland lies in this 'cockpit' and has gone through a violent and tragic history surrounded, as it is, by powerful and avaricious neighbours. Way back in history it was the Swedes who ravished the country [miraculously leaving the famous picture of Our Lady in Czestochowa scarred but otherwise unscathed] and the country, weakened by wars and the usual Slav internal squabbles, was carved up in 1772 by agreement between Russia, Prussia and Austria. In 1793 the same three powers repartitioned the country and the final agreement of 1795 erased the country from the map of

Europe; a political and geographical fact which remained for 146 years. Through brutal repression of the population in this period and exclusive education in Russian, Prussian or Austrian respectively each part became, in effect, simply a part of the occupying nation. All men were forced to serve in the respective armies and a universal apathy and resignation took the place of any pride in nationhood, language or national traditions. The Prussians and Austrians added what we would now call 'ethnic cleansing' to normal repression by systematically re-populating their zones with native immigrants Catherine the Great and the Russians did not indulge in anything so subtle but simply brutally and utterly eradicated the Polish language, religion and traditions.

It was a miracle that after so many generations subjected to such enforced re-education and annexation to other powers the 'spirit of Poland' as it was triumphantly described, still lived and rose again in 1918.

It was into this sort of political and national climate that on February 24th 1904 was born Helena Elzbieta (Elizabeth). She was the only child of doting parents and, by her own admission, was very loved and spoiled, particularly by her proud father. Although it is true that she was the only child of this marriage she had, in fact, nine half siblings from her mother's first marriage which ended with the death of her husband at an early age with the youngest child being only two years old. It was taken for granted that she would marry her brother-in-law if only to keep the considerable wealth already in the family from being shared anywhere else. Circumstances, however, changed all this. A young law student arrived in this close-knit community and a short courtship the young widow was swept off her feet by this even younger stranger and married him instead. He was, in fact, eighteen years her junior and all this took place against the strong and bitter opposition of all her family and started a feud which continued for many years.

Matters did not improve when the young husband proceeded to live in some comfort off the considerable wealth which had been left entirely to the widow. Family fury grew and erupted so that the older children of the first marriage were alienated from their mother and her young husband. Only the three youngest did, in fact, remain with their mother and were brought up with the infant Helena, whose most cherished memories were of her two brothers, Arthur and Maximilian.

Theophil Kozlowski, the young husband and father, continued to live a comfortable and even extravagant life. He studied music at the Berlin Conservatory, enjoyed the arts and generally led the life of a gentleman of wealth and leisure. This continued for seven years with no thought, apparently, to the future.

Helena, in the meantime, was growing up as a pretty, gifted and intelligent child who had inherited her father's love of music and sense of fun. From her mother she had courage, strength and determination as well as a sense of practicality. She attended a private school, the equivalent of a grammar school for girls known throughout Prussia as 'Die Tochterschule'. She had an aptitude for languages and the arts in general but was specially gifted in the use of the written word. She became an accomplished pianist at an early age - a second choice to her favourite instrument, the violin. This, apparently, she did not start to learn from her father but together with another pupil. Since she was always being blamed for his wrong notes she decided to branch out and concentrate on the piano instead.

She enjoyed the company of many friends of various religious denominations and nationalities both from the school and the neighbourhood. Life was safe and happy when suddenly, at the outbreak of war in 1914, all was to change. Her father and all the older step-brothers were called up to join the Prussian army. Mother, young Helena and step sister Martha were left to cope with shortages and rationing until the end of the war when, with and Russia in the throes of revolution, Poland experienced another resurrection.

This came about, first, because in the Great War all three occupying powers suffered defeat. Secondly, the decision of the peace conference in 1919 was to establish the state of Poland and set up its boundaries. To avoid what would now be called 'ethnic cleansing' it was decided by the fledgling Polish government to allow the population to opt for the country of their choice. Those citizens who had Prussian, German or Austrian sympathies were free to opt for that country, allowed to sell up and all their possessions and funds to start a new life in the country of their choice. Those who decided to stay were allowed to do so but had to swear allegiance to the new State, accept citizenship, learn the language if necessary, and so make up the new autonomous state of Poland.

Helena's father chose Poland while all her Siblings opted for Germany. Now at the age of and in her last year at school, ready to take examinations, she was faced with the new political order requiring all education and examinations to be taken in Polish. This presented a formidable problem since, although her father was of Polish origin and spoke the language fluently, he had failed to impart it to his daughter and her 'mother tongue' was, in practice, German She had to adjust, learn the language but still managed to pass her exams with flying colours.

Through all this transition in Poland matters were not made any easier by the raging inflation in the whole of Europe. What little may have remained from her mother's considerable wealth now became exhausted and father had to apply himself to earning a living. He first applied for and was appointed as a church organist in Poznan. This, although most enjoyable, was too much like hard work so he decided to fall back on his legal training. With great confidence and resourcefulness he started a firm of consultants and gave legal advice on insolvency and bankruptcy. This venture established itself quickly and firmly and discovering that good money could be earned with the minimum of genuine effort he settled down to a very pleasant life. Helena was sent on to a college to complete her education but since there was no need for her to earn a living a career was never seriously contemplated.

At the age of seventeen she met, through mutual friends, a young Airman eleven years her senior, and fell in love. Her father refused to allow her to many but eventually did agree so that Helena was married on December 26th 1923, aged nineteen, to Denis Felix Pieczka.

He was from a farming background. The younger of two children, his mother died in childbirth when he was about two years old. His father remarried a girl much his junior and had a large second family. A condition of his marriage was that all the family property - a large farm - had to be made over to his new wife and, in effect and fact, disinherit the two children from his first marriage. They, in turn, found it very difficult to accept their new stepmother because of her tender age (she was only about l5). She had been a playmate and used to play hide and seek with them and skate on the village pond. Now, suddenly, they were expected to call her 'Mother'. Both children were academically bright but it was made clear to them that no further education would be available since all resources had to be kept for the new and growing family.

In 1914, at the age of 21, Denis volunteered for the Prussian army and was sent off to fight on the Eastern front. He spent some time in Finland and also served in the Bicycle Corps where he received his war wound - he fell off his bike into a ditch, cut his upper lip and, to hide the slight scar, sported a moustache which, many years later when such an appendage became too reminiscent of Hitler, he shaved off with detriment to his good looks.

While serving at the front he received a letter from his sister telling him that she had decided to join a convent - the community known as the Grey Sisters or the Order of St.Elizabeth, a nursing and teaching order quite well known on the continent. After her novitiate she was sent to Sweden where she spent 50 very fruitful years working, originally, with Polish children in that country. In co-operation with the Embassy she collected children of Polish immigrants into Sweden from various outlying farms and communities, brought twelve boys and twelve girls into Malmo where the order had purchased a house. There the children were educated and also taught religion and the Polish language. The whole scheme was funded by charity and the now Sister Osea was most resourceful in sending a monthly magazine to Poland and making frequent forays into the mother country to collect funds. After the end of the second World War her work changed to some extent since she became involved in the rehabilitation of survivors from the concentration camps.

Meanwhile, back to 1918, her brother and all the rest of the family opted to stay in the new Poland Denis decided to carve out a career in the Polish Air Force which was just being founded but before he could follow this decision the country went to war with Russia and, under President and General Pilsudzki, the little Polish army took up arms against the mighty Russia, torn with internal conflict of the revolution, and liberated the eastern part of Poland. Having played his part in this military campaign this time as part of the Polish, not the Prussian army - he started in the Air Force which educated him into taking a degree in civil engineering and he became an instructor in the Air Force teaching apprentices in Bydgoszcz - also known in its Germanic form as Bromberg. He was there in 1923 when the marriage took place.

They settled down to married life and on February 26th 1925 a little girl was born - Irene Elizabeth. She was the apple of her grandparents' eye. Two years later another girl arrived and was named Marja. Tragedy struck in the form of convulsions and an extremely high temperature when she was two days old. Meningitis was diagnosed and the whole family was distraught. No expense was trying to find a cure but, without modern medicine, she survived the illness only to retain serious traits of disorder which, nowadays, would be called autism. Very little was known about this at the time and the parents went from one doctor to another seeking help and a cure, even taking refuge in various forms of alternative medicine. The child lived for four years and repeated seizures from one of which she eventually died. These were four traumatic years for the whole family.

Some two years after the death of the first Marja a second one was born - Marja Louise, followed two and a half years later by the birth of the long-awaited son - Stanislaus Andrew Denis - to, apparently, the joy of the whole family (hence the three Christian names). It has been enshrined in family history that Helena's mother, by then seriously ill with cancer, looked at this infant male and prophesied that he would be a handsome man because he had broad shoulders and narrow hips! Unfortunately she was not to see the error of her forecast since she died when he was about six months old, but the sentiments are remembered with great fondness and gratitude by her now senile and still not handsome grandson.

Through all these years there was the constant possibility and threat that the Air Force technical school would be transferred to the eastern part of Poland - and Denis and the family with it. It was still a fact that although Poland was politically one state, the various parts united from years of partition were utterly different in culture, background, language, attitude and general way of life. To bring about genuine unity the authorities had the brilliant idea of transferring civil servants and military personnel from one district to another. By moving those from the west to the east and vice versa and sending the odd ones to the south it was hoped that in the next generation the deep-rooted differences could be reconciled. However, those from the west abhorred the idea of having to live in the east, tainted as it was with Russian history and customs. Those from the east could not easily envisage living in the west which was considered verging on the Prussian and Germanic and tainted by the 'Huns'.

However, in 1937 Denis had to make the choice of moving either to Warsaw or right out east near the Russian border. He chose Warsaw as the lesser of two evils and situated some seven hours' train journey from Bydgoszcz. In spite of great reluctance, the family had to move late in 1937 and the transition was not easy. A comfortable and spacious home, the family's own property, all her friends and widowed father had to be exchanged for a flat on the outskirts of Warsaw; modern and just being developed and occupied mainly by military families and employees of various government ministries, most of them in the same situation of transition.

The family settled down and sent the eldest child to a grammar school and the two younger ones to a kindergarten run by Franciscan nuns - most of whom were refugees from Russia. Threats, rumours and the fear of war increased every day and, as all now know, on the first day of September 1939 Germany invaded Poland and in spite of typically heroic but also suicidal resistance the country was overwhelmed by the Blitzkrieg attack in a matter of days rather than weeks.

On the very first day we sat on the balcony and calmly watched the bombers attacking the nearby airport. As children we felt utterly secure because father was there and with us. On the fifth of September, however, he came home and had a serious discussion with mother before announcing that the Airforce school was being evacuated to Lwow. Apparently all the military personnel had been told they could take their families with them. Father made it clear that as a soldier on active duty the probability existed that he would not be able to assure our future if we moved away from our firm base in Warsaw. He could not say what the future might hold. My mother, therefore, decided to stay in the hope that the war would not last long - "it would all be over by Christrnas" they were saying on all sides.

My Father in his Polish Air force uniform he loved the Air Force

On the fifth of September, therefore, father bade his farewells to his family, joined the school and was transported by train to Lwow while that very night Warsaw was bombed heavily and indiscriminately. No public or private shelters existed but father had been on very good terms with the Mother Superior - a Countess, no less - of the Franciscan order nearby and he had been in touch with her before leaving and commended his family into her care. She duly sent a nun and some assistants to persuade mother to bring the whole family, plus a canary, into the convent cellars. We marched across the new park opposite our flat and on to the convent where the shelter promised to be more secure than simply staying in a flat. Every day we went back for a bath and to keep an eye on the property. Soon the bombing became too intense to allow for such forays into the open. The shelter became a public one and was soon filled to capacity with refugees from all sides; from the east because the Russians had slyly invaded there under the cover of Hitler's declaration of war. Stalin quite blatantly transported the families of anyone in uniform - military, railway, police or scouts - into the wilds of Siberia and thousands who had been evacuated, like father, ended up there. Countless refugees were simply fleeing before Hitler's victorious army.

We learnt many years later that the transport which was to have taken the Airforce school personnel on the fifth of September was bombed to a rapid standstill all returned to Warsaw and, taking up arms, set off on foot to Lwow. Half way there they were told of the Russian advance and the whole company - officers, instructors, men, apprentices and families - managed to cross into Roumania.

Meanwhile Warsaw was declared a fortress to be defended at all costs. It was very heavily bombed and eventually capitulated so that by the end of October the German occupation was complete. During all this heavy fighting all kinds of adventures took place and truly heroic deeds were done. Across the road the convent was a house still in the process of being finished and a young mother, surrounded by elderly relatives went into labour without benefit of doctors or nurses. In desperation, taking their lives into their hands, some people ran through the bombing and strafing to seek help from the convent. This was not a nursing order of nuns and their knowledge of obstetrics was non-existent. Our Helena, being a determined lady, took one of the nuns with her, went to the house and delivered the baby acting both as midwife and godparent at the Baptism of a beautiful little girl. No doubt coincidentally but also quite uncannily and unexpectedly immediately after the birth there was a cease-fire - as though the baby had been a harbinger of peace.

A few days later, against all advice, she decided to go and make sure that the flat was safe, unharmed, not destroyed or pillaged. Commending the children into the care of the good nuns she crossed this large park into territory already being occupied by the Germans. In spite of the fact that others had been shot trying to cross this very open space she ran across and, when in range, shouted in German: "Good morning, boys!" Taken aback by such a greeting they let her through the barricades, she explained the purpose of her visit - to see to the flat, get some warm clothes for the children etc. - and was allowed to go to the flat. Busy packing a few essentials she was interrupted by the entrance of a charming young German officer who, although was much taken by her fluent German and her explanation of her background, then proceeded to search the flat. He soon found father's uniform, informed her - and made her cry - that all Polish officers were dead found his service revolver, a hunting rifle and ammunition possession of which at that time was punishable by death. He offered to dispose of them, they parted good friends and mother set off to return to her children. As soon as she left the house she was arrested as a spy and an anxious day followed with intensive questioning in solitary confinement. Taken at last to the officer in charge it was explained to her what a foolhardy act it had been to be seen talking to the Poles on one side of the park and then crossing over to the other side to be equally friendly to the Germans. There was, after all, a war on and she was lucky to be allowed to go back on promising not to return until the total occupation of the area.

A promise very willingly given. She returned to the great relief of Mother Superior who had sent out for information and been told by the Polish sentries that certainly, the lady had crossed, been seen to have been arrested but they had no further knowledge of her fate. These are the sort of things she tended to do either through lack of fear or some sort of complete trust in the righteousness of her cause.

Even after the total occupation of Warsaw it took a long time for life to resume even the semblance of normality. There was no light, no electricity and no food. Field kitchens were set up by the Germans to feed the population, at the cost of waiting and queuing and taking pot luck. A more than average severe winter set in to add to the worries of no husband, no income, no news of what was going on plus a spectacularly devalued old currency which had to be exchanged for new money - unless you were a Jew, in which case even this was forbidden.

Some of her Jewish school friends had escaped from Germany into Poland and they came to her and asked her to front them in exchanging their old money into new. Nothing loath and backed by her fluency in the language she promptly did so, with no little risk to herself since dealing with Jews in such matters was automatically punishable by death or concentration camp. Her friends duly showed gratitude by helping with food and fuel, much needed in a flat which had survived but was windowless and freezing. Winter and Christmas of 1939 was spent in just one room of the flat with the adults - in effect, mother, my sister and the maid - being allowed to line up at soup kitchens and thus feed the rest of the family Although still in full possessions of the comforts of home we had no knowledge of the whereabouts of father, no idea of what the future might hold and generally entered the new year in a pretty ghastly situation.

Slowly the situation started to be sorted out into a semblance of normality. Overturned trams and ripped-up rails and pavements all used as anti-tank barriers were cleared up and moved by prisoners of war and by Jews rounded up by the Germans from all parts of the city. Those who had fled at the approach of the Germans were gradually returning to find their homes either destroyed or totally looted. The bodies buried all over the city in parks and grass verges were being exhumed, reburied in cemeteries, listed and categorised and families informed wherever possible. It was at this time that we heard that my father's youngest half-brother, aged 18, was among the dead but we never found his grave.

The transport and postal services were gradually being restored and it became apparent that the country was, once again, partitioned. All the territory west of Warsaw which had belonged to Germany before the 1914 - 1918 war was now designated as "Neues Reich". The rest of the country, up to the Russian and Austrian borders, was called the "Generalguwemament". This meant that before one could visit the western part of Poland one had to obtain a passport and visa from the German authorities. Great numbers of inhabitants were uprooted, disowned and resettled into the eastern parts of Europe so that Germans could be housed in the west A great deal of suffering ensued from the tearing apart of families and depriving many of properties held and treasured through generations.

Father's family were given twenty minutes to pack and leave as they were evicted from their home and farm. It was only due to the family's great standing and regard in the community that they were re-settled on a very small and ramshackle farm nearby and were spared the lot of most of their friends and neighbours of being sent to labour camps to the east of Warsaw where conditions were extremely harsh. Old grandfather was in his eighties and they were lucky. Even though life for them was hard throughout the war, they were free. Helena's father was also evicted and disowned but escaped deportation only to have to share a flat with friends, having been refused permission to come to us in Warsaw. She was informed that all the properties in Bydgoszcz had been confiscated and thus any income from them ceased.

Meanwhile the German authorities became obsessed with the fear of a typhoid epidemic in the city. The whole population had to endure anti-typhoid vaccinations which took three weeks to complete with one injection per week over a period of three months. People became terrified by the whole procedure since the shortage of needles meant that only one needle per district was available. Whoever had the misfortune of being at the end of the queue simply had to endure an incredibly blunt needle.

Throughout all this Helena had to maintain the family in some way Stan's reaction to the injections was always a high fever and quite a serious illness and she discovered during this period that volunteers were needed, who were healthy and clean, to offer themselves to the Pasteur institute to feed live lice on themselves. These loveable bugs have to feed on fresh human blood so that they could be used to produce serum for the injections. This may sound incredible and mediaeval but was highly practical and the chosen volunteers were rewarded with butter, eggs, bread, milk and soap. She promptly volunteered and for the next few weeks the family were fed and washed on the back of this bizarre experience.

She had to consider supporting the home and family and the servant still with her for the long-term future. All official posts were being filled with ethnic Germans while those in positions of responsibility were given much more menial tasks with, of course, appropriate falls in salary. The great benefit of any such jobs was that those thus employed were given an identity card marking them as working for the State and under German supervision. These cards were worth their weight in gold since throughout the occupation civilians were regularly rounded up and those without such a card were liable to be transported to Germany for labour in the factories there. This applied to any able bodied person, man or woman, over the age of 14. Helena decided to look for work and approached the Post Office - for no apparently special reason - for work as an interpreter. The pay was low and the hours long and she had to subsidise her income by privately doing translations, writing applications and appeals for those whose relatives and friends had been arrested, giving German lessons and generally doing anything that came along and with which she was able to cope.

Official payment was cash but far more valuable was payment in kind - food. The barter system had been re-invented all over the city. Life was very difficult. People were severely repressed and deprived and all kinds of valuables were being exchanged for food and fuel. All father's civilian clothes were converted into coats and jackets and dresses for the family - the poor man would only have had hats and shoes if he had returned.

The family settled into a routine with correspondence with Sweden on a regular basis but with letters from my aunts being heavily blacked out by the official censor. This was a great worry since there was always the fear that if any of the aunts were being indiscreet then it could have severe consequences for the family. Occasional parcels were very welcome and provided what were very precious luxuries at the time.

The remnants of the Polish army were beginning to get organised into a very efficient underground resistance so that practically on a daily basis there were shootings of German soldiers on the streets of Warsaw. Soon the retaliation by the authorities was to shoot 50 Poles for one German; taken at random off the streets or in night-time raids on private homes. This went up to 100 and eventually to a 1000. All this did not stop the shootings and certainly made no difference to the Germans. Many a time friends came to stay the night since rumour had it that their district would be raided. All this and the general air of repression, violence and cruelty made for a most unsettled life but in spite of it all Helena managed to make the family feel happy and, generally, safe so that apart from missing father and not having any knowledge of his whereabouts (or whether he was dead or alive) we children soon adapted and did not seem to miss all that much in life.

It was not until after the end of the war that Helena revealed that she had been approached by the resistance movement with the proposal to translate and transport documents and occasionally to allow wanted men to hide in our flat. There would have been payment for this generous enough probably to allow her to give up her job. She refused since the penalty if caught was certain death or concentration camp and, of course the splitting up of the family This did not go down well with the resistance and they designated her, the wife of a regular soldier, as unpatriotic: She would eventually have been marked down as anti-Polish and pro-German - a risk she felt she had to take and a decision which was vindicated and supported eventually when we were re-united with father.

In the midst of all this there was suddenly a genuine war going on the middle of Warsaw in what had been made into a Jewish ghetto. From the start of the occupation all the Jews had been gathered up from the city and surroundings and concentrated into one area which was surrounded by a high wall with strictly restricted entry and exits. Extreme cruelty was a daily practice in the ghetto, perpetrated by both Germans and quite a few of the Polish police - the Poles in general do not have a great record of kindness to Jews through the ages. Gradually the ghetto area was restricted and the inhabitants more and more constricted starved and ill-treated until about 1943 they rebelled and there was a full scale war in the middle of the city lasting some three weeks or so. No mercy was shown and the unequal struggle ended in the utter levelling of the ghetto and the death of most of the inhabitants and deportation of the remainder Helena found all this particularly distressing since some of her school time friends had been among the number.

Rumour supported by fact made it clear that the eastern front was rapidly approaching Poland and this became even more obvious when, at the height of the summer, the Germans started packing and their families began to leave for Germany - ostensibly for their holidays. Unrest in the city grew by leaps and bounds and since our fear of the Russians was so great, that it warranted any risk Helena decided to take such a risk and leave Warsaw to go west, to Bydgoszcz. Speaking fluent German certainly helped but things were becoming generally more chaotic so that passes were no longer checked with such care and movement became easier. In the nick of time, days before the now notorious Warsaw uprising, we left our home there - that home which Helena had worked so hard to maintain for father's return - and set off west never to return.

On the 1st August 1944 the resistance rose up against the occupying German forces in Warsaw and a bitter and violent struggle for the city continued for some weeks. The Russian army was on the outskirts of Warsaw, literally within artillery range, and the Polish resistance can be excused (although from history they should have known better) in their confidence that, having risen inside the city and attacked the Germans from within, the Russians would use the opportunity to attack from outside. Instead Uncle Joe used the time to reinforce and rest his army and allowed the Germans and Poles to slaughter each other. This was such an obvious ploy as shown by the Russian refusal to allow the RAF. to drop supplies for the resistance; something the long range would only allow if the supply planes could then land on Russian territory, Permission was refused and not only did all the fighting markedly weaken the German garrison but it also got rid of quite a few Poles who would have proved a problem to the Russians once they, in their turn, had overrun and occupied the country. The casualties in Warsaw were enormous and the city was practically devastated with, of course, our own flat and all that remained of the family chattels being lost as well.

There was little future for us in Bydgoszcz. The only accommodation was in sharing the already shared flat with Helena's father while the comparatively nearby farm of the other grandfather could not house us either and refugees from the east - which, by then, we had become - were not conducive to the safety of those already living on the brink and at the whim of authorities only too ready to confiscate property and transport whole families. In any case, the dreaded Russian bogey was only delayed by the Warsaw interlude and continued rolling west - which we also proceeded to do, as it happened, ended up in Dresden.

Whatever treasures we had managed to save from Warsaw had now to be pruned down to hand luggage. This included our wirehaired foxterrier who had to be left behind while we set with a suitcase each - sizes according to ages and muscles - and going from one town to another partly using the irregular train service or cattle trucks after sitting around on stations for hours and partly on foot, we joined the ever-swelling tide of refugees heading away from the Russian invading hordes. The plan was to get to Sweden eventually and thus take up the standing invitation from our nun aunts there. By then they had been there for so long that they were naturalised Swedes and the country having managed to remain neutral it was an obvious magnet to the homeless.

It seemed a good idea at the time, since distances were not covered in straight lines but where whatever transport took us, to drop in on Dresden where Helena's half-sister, Martha, had a thriving little tobacco business grandiosely named "Zigarrenhaus Schlicke". She received us with open arms when we arrived there in January 1945 but other members of the family were descending on her at the same time and space was scarce. Dresden had become a centre for refugees from all quarters. Partly because the place had never been seriously bombed since it was noted much for its cultural and historical interest rather than anything military. We happened to meet a German lady who asked if we were looking for accommodation and on being told that this was the case and without any more questions or investigation into our honesty or otherwise she offered us a share in her home in a block of flats. These were pre-war and substantial buildings and she lived on the fourth floor with her small son while her husband was serving in the army. She was very kind to us and we shared everything even the meat ration which came from the remains of the lionhouse in the Dresden zoo.

It was there that on the 13th of February, Shrove Tuesday, at about 10.00pm., the air raid warning sounded and we all filed into the cellar according to, by now, well established routine and custom. This time, however, the heavy drone of bombers did not pass on overhead to drop its lethal load on some other city but, instead, destroyed the old part of Dresden which, being mostly built of timber, burned most spectacularly. The 'all clear' duly sounded and everyone went back to their flats and looked with awe at the raging fire in the distance marking the death of the old city.

The German lady's mother-in-law, in her eighties, deaf as a post and sporting an ear trumpet to our secret amusement, lived towards that area and Helena and our host decided to go round to see to her safety, leaving us in bed. It never occurred to anyone that there might be another raid that night. They had hardly left when another alert sounded and before anyone could actually get into the shelters bombs began to drop all around us. The absence of both mothers added to our panic but suddenly, in the thick of the bombing, they both arrived safely having discovered that the old lady had been bombed but had been found shelter in her area.

So there we sat in the cellar, with five or six stories of flats above us and discovered that with true German forethought and efficiency these shelters had been interlinked with one another all along the row of blocks by weakening the adjoining wall so that if one building was hit the people could break through and get in next door. This area of the city was now receiving the full attention of the bombers and the raid continued, it seemed, interminably until, with a tremendous explosion, it became obvious that our block of flats had received a direct hit. Smoke, heat and debris started belching into the cellar aided and abetted by the fact that the intervening walls had now been breached and others were crowding in from both adjoining buildings Utter pandemonium reigned and it was becoming obvious that through heat, smoke and overcrowding the cellar was becoming a mass grave. My sister and Mrs. Richman, the German lady, beat their way out up the stairs to try and rescue our possessions from the flat Helena led us and the lady's son through the flames into the street in spite of dire warnings from everyone else and the obvious fact that the street itself was a sea of fire. It was, in fact what later became known as the 'fire storm' which had already once taken place in

Hamburg and was now sweeping through Dresden. It is a natural phenomenon caused by the presence of intense and widespread heat burning up the very oxygen in the air with the result that a very high wind fans and spreads the flames in a most devastating, spectacular and quite unstoppable manner. It meant, quite literally, running through flames, dodging flying embers, timbers, beams and even sleepers raining down from the burning railway bridge under which we wanted to cross before it collapsed under the weight of its stationary and burning train. The others in the cellar, seeing us survive and run off immediately followed and a mass of humanity simply ran in any direction where the fire seemed to be less intense. We made it, with some difficulty what with fear, holding hands and being still only children, and found comparative calm and safety beyond the bridge.

The only place to go was back to Aunt Martha's which was packed with refugees but unscathed. Lying on the floor and any space available we all spent the rest of the night in restless expectation of yet another raid. This did come early in the morning and the crammed cellar was shaken by a tremendous explosion - a near miss, as we discovered when we found a huge crater just outside the door. It had, incidentally, blown out all the soot from the chimney through the cellar flue with the result that all the lucky survivors looked like black and white minstrels.

The general reaction of those who were refugees, who did not have property or relatives in Dresden but had merely been sheltering there, was to leave and shake the dust of the place off their feet. This, too, it became clear much later, had been part of the purpose of bombing Dresden. The hordes of refugees - on foot and with prams, bicycles and handcarts - blocked all the roads for miles around and prevented any freedom of military movement or reinforcements. People trudged blindly in a vaguely western direction, dazed and at a loss where to go, simply grateful and surprised that they had survived.

Chapter I

From Poland to Bedfordshire

Poland as a nation did not exist in the years before the Great War - the First World War. Politically it was just a part of the huge Austrio-Hungarian Empire with fond memories of its past sovereignty and glory, its own traditions and language and its continuing yearning for independence. As the 'cockpit of Europe' that part of the world was constantly being attacked, occupied and dismembered. The Swedes had occupied it (and a relic of this is still seen in the famous icon of Our Lady of Czestochowa which bears a double scar on the cheek caused, it is said, by the slash of a Swedish sword. When sacking the famous monastery the actual icon became so heavy when loaded up with all the rest of the booty that the horses could not pull the cart. The officer in charge, in sheer frustration - and all expletives have been deleted from the traditional account - took his revenge on the picture and abandoned the load).

The Russians were constantly nibbling at the eastern frontiers and the Germans or their predecessors acquiring territories on the western side. In 1918 the peace treaties re-established this split state of Poland with all its deep-rooted divisions between east and west. The population had to 'opt' for a nationality so that those in the east could remain 'Russians' while those in the west could opt for remaining 'German'. Those who chose to be 'foreign' could remain in the country as more or less welcome aliens while if they opted to be Poles they were there by right. Ethnic cleansing is, thank God, a comparatively modern way of solving such problems.

My mother's father was a civil servant, a sort of court official, and to make sure he kept his job he had to opt to be Polish - even though his roots were pretty Germanic, as was his mother tongue. Her mother was even more German and of quite a noble and wealthy lineage (!) (the family boasted several carriages and a full stable of horses) but through her marriage became a Polish citizen without actually ever being able to master the intricacies of that language.

My Grandfather was a civil servant – in the middle of this picture with my Father and my Mother and the rest of my siblings – Maria – Louise after making her first Holy communion

My father's family was more earthy. They were farmers, also in the west of Poland and had no problems about opting to be Poles - they were keen to do so and were (all of them) genuinely bi-lingual. My mother, on the other hand, had to polish up her Polish when she married. She became genuinely bi-lingual but betrayed her roots by never actually unconsciously, intuitively, counting under her breath in anything but German. It is a very good test as to which language one is actually most at home with: If you count your change in English then it is a sure sign that you actually think in that language and are most at ease in it.

They were married (with an age difference of 11 years - my mother being a mere 19) late in 1923 and lived in Bydgoszcz or its Germanic equivalent of Bromberg where my father was an instructor in the Air Force with a steady and well paid job, good prospects and an ingrained habit and ambition of providing for the future and, eventually, returning to the land as the heir to a flourishing farm.

They had three daughters of whom the second died in infancy. Finally, apparently to great and universal rejoicing, they produced a son in 1935: me. Born with his right eye shut for a week, long, black hair and, as my mother always delighted in telling anyone who might be listening, an 'ugly baby'. The eye opened of its own accord, the hair - as so often happens with babies - thinned out and became mousy and my maternal grandmother, who died some six months after my birth, has always remained very high in my estimation for reportedly maintaining that this baby would grow into a fine figure of a man because he had wide shoulders and narrow hips!

My parents with their first born my sister Irene Elizabeth

My sister Maria-Louise and me – she has always looked after me

Early in 1939, with the clouds of war gathering, my father was transferred to the Air Force college in Warsaw. Off he went, in the line of duty, to be followed much more reluctantly by his wife and family. The reluctance was a very natural one on the part of anyone born and bred in the western regions of Poland. Warsaw was the capital but it belonged to 'the east' and as near to being Russian as made no difference with the people there equally 'different', to put it charitably. The generations of partition have even now not been lived down and there remains a distinct distrust between the east and west. The family settled in a large flat opposite a park on the outskirts of Warsaw and this is more or less my first memory of life.

Some fortunate souls claim they can remember their tender infancy or even the cosy life in the womb. I have a deep suspicion of such claims and reckon they simply rely on reports and stories of their elders and betters. I do remember that dad became the proud owner of a car - quite unusual at that time, especially for a humble Warrant Officer - a dark red Fiat which was promptly used for a holiday trip just before the outbreak of war. An abiding memory is a visit to the salt mines in Wieliczki where a chapel had been formed from crystal salt deep underground and from where I brought back a salt cross which I insisted on licking - a healthy taste for salty things still with me. But the boundary between memory and folklore remains vague. What, at that age, does one really remember and what comes through the stories and reminiscences of one's elders? Certainly, I do clearly remember the start of the war even if details may well have been filled in since through one's own imagination, the facts of history and the tales of others.

The war in Poland started on September 1st and my father left Warsaw on the 5th. The Air Force college was evacuated but everyone said with the greatest confidence that the war would be over in a matter of weeks rather than months and everything would return to normal. Just in case, however, the powers-that-be took the unusual step of paying the Air Force personnel their month's salary in advance and in real silver coins of the realm - with a picture of a be whiskered President Pilsucki on one side and a genuine and crowned eagle on the other. One of these coins still serves me even now as an attachment to my car keys. My father's pride and joy - the Fiat , not me - was requisitioned for military use and we still have, to this very day, the official receipt by which we could claim it back after the war; or its equivalent in hard cash. The whole Air Force college wandered off in a pretty disorganised manner and was soon scattered. Dad's own wanderings and adventures through Europe and eventual arrival in England form another of the innumerable stories of war. To all practical intents and purposes he ceased to exist in my life for the next five years or so and it was eventually more or less generally accepted - although devoutly hoped otherwise - that he was 'missing, presumed dead' as so many others.

The German 'Blitzkrieg' was, obviously, not aimed personally at me; it just felt like it. For that matter, all through the war people were bombing me; Germans at this time, Russians in 1944 and the British, Americans and even the French through the latter part of 1944 and most of 1945. As far as I know the Japanese never actually had any such evil designs on me. We lived quite close to the airport which by the nature of things was one of the prime targets. I do remember bombs falling in the park opposite and shrapnel lying about in weird shapes and sometimes even still hot from the explosion. I also remember horses - still very much part of the military machine in Poland (and even of the German Army which, it is reliably reported, took all of twenty thousand with them for transport - the mind boggles at the thought of providing food, shelter and care for them, not to mention the delight of rose growers at the manure thus freely available - when, a few years later, they attacked Stalingrad) - being wounded and lying in the park and being killed off by the locals who carved off prime bits and pieces since horsemeat was, and continues to be, quite a normal part of the meat-eaters' diet on the continent.

It seemed wise to move a bit further afield. On the other side of the park there was a convent and hospital run by the same order of nuns that three of my father's sisters had joined (although they were based in Sweden). We were thus *'personae gratae'* there and decided to move in for the duration of the actual bombardment. The place was just that much further from the airport and there was the pious hope that they would not, surely, bomb a hospital. The battle for Warsaw did not last very long and neither the hospital nor our flat were hit or damaged. We soon moved back and nothing more traumatic happened than the actual occupation, German armies marching in and soldiers searching every house and confiscating my father's ceremonial 'dagger' which formed part of his dress uniform but was considered to be an offensive weapon.

The fact that my mother spoke fluent German and we ourselves had a decent knowledge of it seemed to serve more to persuade the searchers that they were 'liberating' the populace than making them suspicious that we were spies. Because of the history of Poland it was not all that unusual for German to be spoken even in the eastern parts. Certainly there was no widespread brutality, rape or pillage at that time. But then the front line troops of any army are not prone to such extremes. They are far too busy making their conquests safe and watching their backs. Far more likely that the next wave of occupying forces would have more leisure, incentive and inclination for such behaviour.

My strongest memory of that time is that at last my frequent stomach aches were taken seriously and I was trundled off to the hospital and found to have a very dodgy appendix. For ages I had complained of pains but, no doubt coincidentally, they usually occurred when cabbage was on the menu; which at that time was rather frequent. I have never liked cabbage before or since but was always made to eat it up and a tummy ache was not accepted as an excuse. Eventually, however, my mother decided to call my bluff. I was taken to the doctor and duly justified when they kept me in and operated immediately; none of this modern keyhole surgery at that time. It was a big operation and the patient was not allowed to eat or drink for two days and spent over a week in bed with a bolster under his knees so as not to stretch or break the wound. There is a tiny but infamous photograph of this little fellow lying in a deckchair wearing just pyjama bottoms and enjoying something from a cup; presumably non-alcoholic.

Sun bathing for medicinal use I might add – notice the sun glasses and a nice cup of tea

Quite early on in the war we moved to a smaller flat more in the centre of the town and my mother found work in the general Post Office. This, like all the amenities, was now being run by the Germans - soldiers in uniform but with expertise background so that, in fact, they were simply managers in the army; like army doctors, dentists etc. They clearly had to employ natives and the ability to speak and write German was a great advantage. Technically such work may well fall under the heading of co-operating with the enemy. But there was little choice for my mother. Obviously there was no salary nor pension from the Polish Air Force and there were three kids wanting to be fed and clothed. She remained in this job - dealing mainly with misdirected and lost letters and parcels - until 1944 and we became what would now be known as 'latchkey kids'.

My theory is that children are far more resilient than people realise or give them credit for and that the modern attitude that everything that happens in one's early years, especially the bad things, leave an indelible trauma does nothing but stress those negative experiences and leads people to 'expect' to have such traumas. Certainly, there are effects and bad memories and continuing links which trigger off reactions but people in general and children in particular can and do live in the most evil and appalling circumstances and cope, learn to adjust, and survive. Either that theory makes some sense or I was then and have continued to be a most insensitive character. Maybe, of course, the reason why I tend to be a rather 'odd bod' now is the result of the experiences and traumas of the next few years and I have spent the last 60 years fooling myself that I am 'normal'!

Education started at the decent age of six and I remember trudging off to school with a leather satchel on my back containing a slate, the odd elementary reading book and an apple. A damp sponge (used for cleaning said slate) dangled on the outside of the satchel on a piece of string. All vastly different from what one sees nowadays when even infants emerge from four-wheel drive vehicles festooned with anoraks and bags as if going off on an arctic expedition.

School started at 8.00 a.m. and finished at 1.00 p.m. No school milk nor school dinners; a meagre sandwich and the apple seemed quite enough. We, my sisters and myself, set off after our mother left for work and came back to await her return to have the main meal, do the usual things done by families at that time (no T.V., not much radio) playing, reading, bit of homework and bed. I acquired a habit - very useful when learning to read - of reading everything I saw; shop and street names, inscriptions on lorries, signposts, advertisements etc. A habit which is still with me so that even when driving I know that I have just passed an Eddie Stobard lorry from Cumberland and that a left turn would have taken me to Yardley Gobion in two miles and that 247 motorists had been prosecuted for speeding through Wing in the past month. But I was no intellectual giant in any way and painfully learned to write - with many a squeak to set one's teeth on edge - on the slate. I have no particularly clear recollection of the school, the teachers or the other pupils; perhaps a blessed and self-imposed oblivion or just my normal obtuseness.

In spite of the war and occupation things went on more or less as normal - or, at least, my memories are not constantly scarred by world shaking events. There is no knowing what life and childhood would have been like if there had been no war, if my father had been part of the family and if we had continued in what was; comparatively, a comfortable situation. But we had a home and security and the normal life and traditions and experiences of childhood. Christmas was always something special with the main celebration on Christmas Eve with beer soup and carp to spoil it. Because it was a fasting and abstinence day there had to be no meat; and custom had it that the evening meal consisted of beer soup (which I found tolerable) followed by grilled carp (which I hated) with potatoes, vegetables etc, ending with poppy-seed pudding and cake (which I loved). The carp we used to buy in the market a few days before Christmas, alive, and keep them swimming around in the bath to be treated as pets by us kids and fed on bread crumbs. It is only quite recently that I was told the reason for this: apparently fresh carp have a distinctly muddy taste and have to be kept in clear water for a few days to flush out their systems. And through all these years I thought it was just to provide us with a bit of harmless fun, which just goes to show, again, that we are never too old to learn. The said carp were then taken out of the bath on Christmas Eve morning and battered on the head with a heavy weight until dead. Then cleaned, gutted and coated in flour etc and eventually grilled on the pan. Apparently the nervous system is such that heat makes the bits of very dead fish jump in and often even out of the frying pan; great to watch by a blood thirsty lad. Christmas presents were few in comparison to what is given now, but they were laid under the Christmas tree and could only be opened when we returned from midnight Mass.

With no television and with radio just a source of music and censored news one wonders what people did at that time to enjoy themselves. I remember walks, playing with neighbourhood kids and getting into mild trouble, having white mice which were so tame they lived in my pocket but which increased and multiplied so alarmingly that eventually they all gnawed their way our of the cage and had to be thrown out into the wide world. We always had a dog and even a tortoise which, when taken out into the park, could move amazingly quickly when not watched and was always getting lost. He eventually killed himself by falling off the third storey balcony of our flat on to the pavement. Like all our deceased pets, he got a Christian burial. I myself was being prepared for first Confession and Holy Communion but never made it before we actually had to leave Warsaw. I was eventually re-prepared, this time in German, while in Gusten - see later - and actually made my first Confession before again having to hit the road. I still have the card stating that this event took place. I was, eventually, again instructed for First Holy Communion, this time in English, and made it at the advanced age of 11 plus. I'm not sure what this proves about my mental powers or my spiritual development.

Again, at the risk of repeating myself, I am sure that children are far more resilient than this modern age and attitude admits. There was no talk of traumas or counsellors. Life and its hardships and cruelties were taken for granted and compensated for by making life ordinary and 'normal'. I suspect that all this modern talk of how children in, say, Belfast, are traumatised; how refugees and inhabitants of war-torn territories will never be the same; how children must even be sheltered from the normal deaths and tragedies in the family and even the bad news of disasters and cruelties throughout the world does them no favours in the end. Certainly this would not apply to children who had been personally brutalised and the multitudes who suffered indescribable pain, torture or loss. But even in the worst cases time is a great healer and even the most painful experiences of the past should be allowed to get fuzzy, to say the least, through time rather than be raked up, analysed and riveted on one's consciousness for ever. The most evil things happened and still continue to happen and probably do have some effect; but why try to pin-point this or even use it as an explanation of the oddities, quirks, mental attitudes or even extreme reactions and criminal tendencies of adults many years later?

I do remember nearly setting the house on fire because of my preoccupation with fire and matches. The ceiling was blackened and carpet spoilt and I decided to go out into the wide world rather than face the wrath of my mother on her return from work. I was caught not too far down the road, faced the expected wrath, went to bed without supper but have still retained my delight in bonfires and even (with care) pouring petrol on reluctant flames.

Another experience which left, literally, a scar was the result of blatant disobedience. Playing on some ruins which had been caused by the bombing was banned but also exciting. One day I slipped and fell, embedding a pebble into my right temple, bleeding profusely and causing my mother to have to come rushing from work to my rescue. The doctor, apparently, said that if the damage had been a fraction of an inch (centimeter?) or so lower it could have penetrated into what he charitably called my brain and could well have killed me! Obviously, I survived but still bear an interesting small scar.

Another, and far more sad, experience was the death of our little dog. A kind of Jack Russell of no particular pedigree he had the heart of a lion. Nothing scared him and we used to rush around together pressing all the buttons in entrances to high rise flats so that all the occupants buzzed back together while we made tracks down the road. In the winter, probably of 1941, he acted as a sledge puller with four or five of us on board. It is probable that the strain was too much for the little dog. One morning after such exertions, he was not himself. He was vicious and foamed at the mouth and went to bite my ankle - difficult through a high leather boot which was the normal footwear for that season.

Perhaps he even got through fractionally; I have a certain fear or phobia of water. Not pronounced enough to make me avoid baths when absolutely necessary but certainly a reluctance initially to plunge my hand into a sink and finding little pleasure in just wallowing in a hot bubble bath; could be just a touch of rabies with its hydrophobia. There was no Rolf Harris nor animal refuges, no animal welfare societies and no free vets. I had to have him put down, there and then, and before going off to school.

Taking him on a long lead I wandered out into the street to look for a soldier with a gun. Having found one I asked him to shoot the dog; which he did, reluctantly but realising it was inevitable. One shot from his pistol and the poor little chap gave a yelp, buried his head in the snow and was dead. My pathetic and tearful reaction then has not changed since; I still insist on being present when any of my animals, even goats, pigs or ducks, get the merciful chop and I still weep bitterly and feel most embarrassed in front of the vet or knacker's man. Fortunately, they are always very kind and understanding even if they do go off convinced they have been dealing with a proper weed.

My love and respect for animals started even at an earlier age than this.

Reflection

Heavenly Father, It is we humans, masters and custodians and guardians of creation who have the duty and privilege and the ability to care for animals as God intended.

When there is cruelty and neglect, carelessness or sheer lack of thought or consideration of animals it is demeaning, shameful to ourselves. It belittles us, makes us less worthy of respect. We are failing to act according to our nature. For reasons of convenience, sport, pleasure or profit or innumerable other motives we use our intelligence and our will to lower our own dignity in the sight of God, our neighbour and – yes – the animal world itself.

Father Stan – from the Genesis of Animals and Men [The Ark 2004].

Living as a child in occupied Warsaw did mean that one heard of terrible atrocities and even witnessed brutality and death. Not every day at first hand but often enough to make one accept such things as just part of life. German soldiers were more and more often gunned down in the street by 'Resistance Fighters' - and retaliation took the form of men being rounded up in ever larger numbers, whipped and beaten into lorries and taken away; mostly to be never heard of again. Then, as now, I fear that such resistance was counter productive. The evil and inevitable retaliation meant that more and more men and even young boys were shot out of hand - eventually 100 for each German killed. One Sunday morning there was the unmistakable sound of gunfire just below our balcony and a German soldier was dying on the street. The usual sirens of German police Lorries were heard within minutes, the usual scramble of men trying to make themselves invisible, the inevitable round-up, questioning and searches followed. Within an hour or so everything was back to normal - it seemed distant, impersonal, not actually affecting 'us' in our closed little family unit.

My Mother in 1939

More disturbing was the trip to school, on a tram, past the Jewish ghetto where one could see in over the wall the squalor and distress of men, women and children in the enclosed and guarded area. One heard terrible stories of cruelty and occasionally saw baiting and beatings in the street. One morning a little lad was caught trying to get out through a tiny drainage hole in the wall which even in his emaciated state was just too small to allow him to negotiate. A soldier beat and kicked him back into his ghetto and I do remember being grateful - even smug - that, for some reason, I was not in that area, did not have to wear a yellow star, was not starving and beaten and despised. But a seven, eight year old did not reason things out, could not grasp the injustice and prejudice in a climate when it was difficult enough to have the essentials of life and simply keep out of trouble. Eventually, as all know, the whole of that area was flattened by bombs and explosives which we used to hear and see every night for several weeks until all those Jewish families were either killed or transported elsewhere. It was something frightening happening to other people at the other side of town.

By 1944 things were getting pretty rough. The Russians were steadily advancing while the Resistance was getting stronger and braver and threatening a general uprising to oust the occupying German forces. Being 'westerners' we had an intuitive fear and dread of the Russians and the nearer they got the stronger was the urge to go west; to go back to Bydgoszcz where our roots were as well as a house and relatives and a false feeling of more security. It was becoming clear to most that the Germans were not going to win this war but there was always the hope that the war would somehow end while the Russians were still on their eastern side of Poland and the west would, possibly, return to its 'status quo'. In addition to all this, we had an ace up our sleeve - we could, eventually, take refuge in Sweden; a neutral country and the sort of Mecca which beckoned us and which we could hope to reach, if necessary, because of our connections there.

My father came from a large family. He and one sister had a common mother who died when they were quite young.

His father then married a much younger woman, only just a bit older than his two children. They produced six or seven more offspring but with the result that the two from the first marriage became somewhat estranged. The eldest daughter became a nun in an order which had missionary convents and hospitals and homes in Sweden. In due time, she was joined there by two of her half sisters who also became nuns. Throughout the war we received very welcome food parcels from Sweden as well as letters. The parcels contained such delicacies as chocolate, coffee, cocoa, sardines - and prunes! But the letters were always heavily censored so that all reference to our father being alive and well in England were erased. We feared he was dead; the nuns in Sweden knew he was well and he, through them, knew where we were and what we were doing. If the worst came to the worst we knew that we would be welcome in Sweden if, in one way or another, we could make our way there.

With the situation in Warsaw getting fraught we decided to up sticks and move back to Bydgoszcz. All the furniture and most personal effects had to be left behind. My main loss was a stuffed horse! Made some years before from a genuine brown and white calf which had died on grandfather's farm, with a wooden and most realistic head and leather harness, the whole thing was set on rockers and was my pride and joy. We left at the end of July and the infamous Warsaw uprising started on August 1st with much bloodshed and destruction. Heroic in many ways but playing straight into the Russians' hands who calmly halted just out of canon-shot on the outskirts of the city and allowed the Germans and Poles to slaughter each other before marching in without opposition - before adding injury to insult by rounding up what was left of the Resistance and transporting them into the depths of Russia.

We stayed in Bydgoszcz in my maternal grandfather's flat in cramped and unsatisfactory circumstances. The only relief was being able to spend quite a lot of time on the other grandfather's farm (a small affair now that he had been dispossessed of his own property which had been given to immigrant Germans. In some ways he was lucky to have been given a much smaller and run-down patch from which he could just about manage to eke out a living. Many others were simply chased off their land and given nothing.) I would like to think I helped with the harvest by being allowed to ride the one horse as he hauled the wagon and drove the threshing machine. I used to ride bare back on this very skinny nag of whom I became very fond and still remember getting quite a sore backside. I regularly followed the chickens to watch them lay an egg so I could drink it, raw, while still warm. I drank warm, frothing milk straight from the one cow and insisted on lugging a cat around in my spare time in spite of constant warnings from my grandmother (benevolent, bemused by this city kid and nearly stone deaf) that she - the cat - was heavily pregnant. The result was that one night I woke up in my bed with mother and four fit kittens and a bit of a mess. She had decided that the big feather bed would make for a most comfortable maternity ward. To keep me out of their hair, I suspect, my other job was to watch over the cow grazing on the ample grass near the railway line. The cow probably had enough native common sense to keep off the line when trains came by while I used to watch the wagons trundling by loaded with tanks and guns and military equipment and personnel and rolling over and flattening the small coins I had placed on the rails to make them suitable for playing tiddlywinks. Presumably, if the trains had been going faster, this could have derailed them and I would have been classed as a saboteur!

It may well be the usual magic of recollection but all my memories of the farm are of glorious weather in the summers when I used to stay there. 'Helping' with the harvest (no combine harvesters) and the threshing, raking up the straw by, again, sitting on this poor old skinny nag while he pulled a rather primitive rake, being told by my very old-fashioned grandfather when I stripped down to shorts and no shirt that: " *Madmen run around naked while half madmen went around half naked*". Winter or summer he always wore a thick flannel shirt buttoned up to the top and sleeves rolled down. He was a gruff old man with a heart of gold and lived to a ripe old age of 95, dying in the 1950's. His father had had the farm before him and died at 93 - indirectly from drink! The story goes that he was a short and stocky man and probably physically the strongest man in the village; but he liked his drink. One day a cartload of timber got bogged down in the mud and he volunteered, for a bottle of vodka, to get under the cart and lift it up sufficiently for the horses to draw it out. He did this successfully, got his bottle, drank it and promptly dropped dead. It seems as good a way to go as any but if longevity is hereditary then my prospects of being a diamond jubilarian are rosy - downright frightening.

My grandmother was stone deaf and ruled the household with a rod of iron. She must, however, have had a soft spot for this grandson (step-grandson, really) who was a despised 'townee'. She allowed me regularly to raid the chicken nesting boxes and drink raw eggs, put home-made butter on fresh baked bread with a trowel and eat cheese even between meals. Restrictions on what livestock farmers could have and how much milk had to be delivered to the authorities, how much butter, how many eggs, were imposed with great severity. She was a genius at making chickens disappear when the farm was inspected and somehow got away with ridiculous claims as to the amount of milk which was actually produced. There also, in this euphoric memory, always seemed to be trees loaded with cherries, apples and incredibly juicy pears.

In the summer of 1943 I actually was stricken with foot and mouth disease! Cattle used to (and still do) get this regularly and wholesale slaughter was not practised – not as now. I caught it, according to a rather surprised doctor, by either drinking milk straight from a suspect cow or/and from my habit of chewing blades of grass, straw etc when wandering around. The illness did not affect my feet! But large and painful sores appeared in my mouth and I ran quite a high temperature. It was not suggested that I should have been put down but I did have to live on boiled milk, mashed potatoes and stewed apple for two weeks or so.

After the summer holidays I always had to return to the city, back to school and normal town life. There we did not starve but eggs, milk and butter were a rare luxury and I only enjoyed more than my ration because I traded in my meat and sausage portions with the rest of the family.

The greatest benefit of wandering off heading 'west' was that from June 1944 until my arrival in England in July 1946 I never went to any sort of school. What effect this has had on my general education makes the mind boggle and would horrify any Ofsted inspector.

The Russian advance did not, as history shows, stop at Warsaw or even Bydgoszcz. Near the end of 1944 it was obvious that unless we moved west again we would be engulfed and have no hope of reaching Sweden. There was no proper place for us to live where we were so we set off again, with even less goods and chattels; just a suitcase each. The heartbreak for me this time was leaving our dog behind. He was a wire-haired foxterrier who used to sit up and beg for hours on request and wear a scarf and sunglasses. He knew something was up. On the last night he insisted on sleeping with me on the bed; something he never did before. In comparison to what my mother had to leave behind and all her worries for the future this was a trivial loss. On the other hand, I was a thick kid of nine and fond of dogs and as selfish as such kids usually are.

We set off, mostly by train, for Dresden to stay with Aunt Martha. She was a half sister of my mother and she and her husband were comfortably off with no children and a rather superior tobacco shop in that city. My maternal grandmother had had seven children before her husband died. She remarried a much younger man, much against her own family's wishes. He was a gifted musician who never quite reached his potential. They had one daughter, my mother, who was brought up with only two of her half brothers since the others had, by then, grown up and left home. Poor old Martha got quite a shock when we appeared on her doorstep. The letter warning her of our 'visit' had never arrived. To her credit, she rallied well and put us up for a week or so before we actually found a flat. She was a kind lady with an even more gentle and kind husband but four extra bodies was a lot to put up with. The idea was that the whole arrangement would be pretty temporary since letters had gone off to Sweden planning our further progress and eventual migration to this neutral and utopian haven.

Dresden had never been bombed. It had nothing of a military nature in it except for a factory making optical lenses, telescopes and binoculars (which, of course, also included bombing sights, sniper telescopes and U-boat periscopes). It was packed with refugees from all quarters who all felt safe from the general and regular 'carpet' bombing of most large towns and cities. The only bombs recorded were a few weeks before we arrived when a stricken plane had dumped its load on to the cemetery and dug up a few graves. Precautions, however, were still taken ever night when sirens (as a matter of record and interest these were sounded the other way round to the warnings and 'all clears' in England) announced the approach of waves of bombers just before they could be heard approaching. Everyone went into cellars and air raid shelters, the bombers passed overhead to bomb Berlin and Hamburg and anything else on the way. We all went back upstairs to bed at the 'all clear' and listened to the empty bombers going back before dawn. There was a very distinct difference in the sound as also between British and American planes. There was also the practice that radio stations suspended the usual programmes to give reports of how many planes were going over, where they were at any given time and actually stating that they were now overhead. They then closed down - presumably with the broadcasters scuttling into shelters - only to return when the danger or actual raid was over.

In this atmosphere of false security we hung around waiting for something to develop. We shared a flat with a lady and her son about my own age. People were very kind and more than willing to share what little there was. Her husband was somewhere on the eastern front and her mother-in-law was an old lady living in the old part of Dresden and mainly memorable because she was stone deaf but used one of those historic ear trumpets into which one yelled while she either did some lip reading or else just guessed at what was being said. I celebrated my tenth birthday and was given, from some hidden treasures somewhere, a red model racing car with tools so I could remove the tiny wheels and generally take it to pieces before putting it together again. Apart from that we just stooged around and visited poor old Aunt Martha. I can still remember the unique smell of their tobacco shop which grandly boasted the title of *'Zigarrenhaus Schlicke'* - Schlicke being the surname of the proud proprietors.

Shrove Tuesday, February 13th 1945, followed the normal pattern of being a carnival day in preparation for the season of Lent. That night the usual drone of bombers sent us down to the basement fully convinced that after an hour or so we could return safely to our beds. This time, however, the bombs fell in profusion on the far part of Dresden, the old city with predominantly timber buildings and when the wave of bombers retreated we could see the area burning fiercely. My mother and our landlady decided to go off and check on the old lady while the rest of us went up to bed, convinced that the attack was over. Within an hour or so the next wave of bombers arrived and accurately dropped their lethal load on our part of the town. There was a mad scramble back into the cellar and the two ladies, having found no trace of the old dear, just managed to arrive back in time to join us. Huddled in the cellar one could tell by the eerie whistle when a bomb was going to strike in the near vicinity; and strike they did this time. With hindsight it is now obvious that the bombs were more incendiaries than explosives. The whole row of five story houses was hit repeatedly and set alight and the typically German efficiency and foresight came into play.

The cellars were arched and strong and deep so that they withstood the rubble above. They were also linked with each other in the whole road by a specially weakened connecting wall so that if one cellar became intolerable one could break into the next one to escape. They were equipped with bags of sand and huge butts of water and the external doors were specially strengthened. We were the last in the row; all the others quickly broke through one into another and ended up crowding ours to suffocation. A peep through the heavy metal doors into the street showed that there was nothing but flames fanned into violence by a tremendous wind - now known to war scientists as a fire storm caused by so many incendiaries consuming all the oxygen. It became obvious that the whole heaving mass of humanity in the cellar would either burn or suffocate. The future looked short and bleak and panic was not far away.

The regulation barrels of water and buckets of sand were useless in this situation but someone soaked a blanket in water and wrapped it round this little fellow near the door and threw him out into the street through the curtain of flame. That was me; so there I stood outside with fire everywhere and not a soul in sight. I became very vociferous and the penny dropped that where I could go and survive and even yell others could follow. All the occupants of the cellar poured through the door and we all got out; only to be faced by a fiery blizzard and nowhere special to go. A railway bridge nearby spanning the road held a burning train and huge bits of metal and burning railway sleepers were flying through the air like matchsticks. It seemed a good idea to move off before the bridge collapsed and sealed that bit of road. We all managed and people fled away from the fire into the part of the city which still looked safe.

Fortunately, this was in the right direction for our aunt's domain where we arrived, singed, bedraggled, traumatised and without even a suitcase, just in time to take shelter from the next wave of bombers which, by now, had an unmissable target gloriously illuminated by all the flames. Back we crowded, this time into her cellar, with anyone else who happened to be there and sat through another series of explosions. One seemed particularly near but the house survived and the attack eventually came to a gradual end, the drone of planes diminished and vanished and people started emerging into a city which was now burning from end to end. We all looked like black and white minstrels since, apparently, the direct hit went down the chimney and covered us all with soot. There seemed to be nowhere else to go, the planes had gone and dawn was breaking so that it was reasonable to hope that the raid had come to an end. The howling wind had dropped and we retraced our steps to the original cellar to try and retrieve our belongings.

The whole row of houses had collapsed but the curved ceilings of the cellars had held. By judicious digging we found our emergency suitcases - singed brown by the heat (and I still have the small one which was my responsibility) - but there was no hope of finding anything from the flats up above. My greatest loss was the model car which I had only had for a week or so. The routine set up by weeks of practice had come into its own. We each and always had an emergency suitcase containing bare essentials to take down into the cellar. These we all recovered. My mother had all our 'wealth' in money stitched into her corset and since Dresden held no future prospects of anything we were prepared, not to say forced, to travel light. We joined the masses of people trudging aimlessly out of the city and heading - naturally - west and away from the advancing Russian army.

This, apparently, was part of the allied strategy in bombing Dresden. Nothing much of military value had been destroyed but the roads were choked for many miles with refugees in a state of shock and going nowhere; but causing utter confusion and blocking any possibility of military movement or reinforcement or deployment. It was an endless and weird procession in total silence that set out through the ruined city and its suburbs. Suitcases, boxes, bundles were carried while a few fortunate people had a pram or a handcart to take their luggage. There was no rush, no panic. We looked in wonder at street after street of rubble with people digging for survivors or just sitting there blankly in a state of shock. The zoo - which we had visited a week or so earlier - had been destroyed and strange birds were flying about as dazed and lost as was the human population. The dangerous animals had, apparently, been shot but odd eagles and other birds of prey had to find their own food and seemed to be cruising around looking for it. It was quite common to see large parts of bodies being dragged out of the rubble; naked usually since, apparently, bomb blast strips as well as dismembers. At seeing this for the first time my mother made the immortal comment that it must have been a butcher's shop; until she realised, and was never to forget her bizarre *faux pas,* that it was part of a human body.

This bombing of Dresden, just one night of chaos, has had plenty of publicity ever since and the estimates of those killed is anything up to two hundred thousand. I still think that poor old Bomber Harris should not be blamed for it. By this stage of the war this was no more of a brutality than anything else and in the climate of opinion at that time it was perfectly acceptable. Looking back it does appear very different but from my usual selfish point of view it just shows that 'they' had missed me yet again. Before this event as well as often afterwards it does seem that by the law of averages I should not have survived. Which is rather frightening since it raises the question whether I was preserved for some special reason or was it just pure luck?

A few miles and hours out of the city - which, everyone was convinced, would become a target again that night - people started to stop and rest in the countryside and generally the solid procession thinned out. What we knew were American planes - which generally did the daylight bombing raids - flew high overhead but were no threat to mere pedestrians. There was no attempt to bomb or strafe the refugees. One would like to think this was due to humane reasons but could equally have been an acknowledgement of the fact that the job of blocking all traffic was being efficiently done already. But the obvious question now arose as to where we were going. Sweden was a long way away and we had had no proper communication or any idea of how to get there in those circumstances. We had run out of aunts in Germany and seemed destined for one of the refugee camps being set up in various places to house these, literally, tens of thousands of women, children and old men.

I have always liked military bands and continue to do so; especially the German ones with no woodwind but with the 'Glockenspiel'. When staying in Bydgoszcz we visited my grandmother's grave - the one who opined at my birth that I would grow up into a fine figure of a man! - I ran off to watch a military funeral with full pomp and ceremony. It turned out to be the funeral of a young man of 20 who had been wounded on the Russian front by grenade shrapnel. Rumour always had it, rightly or wrongly, that the Russians used poisoned hand grenades so that a wound would eventually fester and kill. His brother had, apparently, been killed just a few months previously at the same front. All this we learned from their parents who stood at the graveside in great distress. They had come from a place near Magdeburg called Gusten and told us that they only had the two boys and they had been in the SS, which need not be as terrible as it may sound since the SS was akin to the Guards; a select corps of men serving in the armoured brigades. It did not always follow that they were the political and inhuman monsters who were responsible for the racist extermination policies. His parents told us that they now had an empty house and if we were ever in need we should not hesitate to come to them for help. It was the sort of exchange of names and addresses people get into on casual acquaintance on holidays - no real intention on either side to keep in touch.

Yet now this was the only place left for us to go. Walking most of the way, hitching the odd few miles on goods trains, we eventually reached Gusten and, utterly unannounced, knocked on their door. They were genuinely delighted to see us! Shocked by our state and our story of being bombed in Dresden, but ready to share their home with us. He was a retired carpenter, they had a four bedroom house with a large vegetable garden on the outskirts of a small town which boasted the addition to its name of " Anhalt" or 'junction'. It was the hub of the railway system in that part of the world and the sidings and sheds were within a stone's throw of their row of houses. We settled down and shared their rations and soon took part in all the local activities to augment the food supply. We kids worked on the local farms weeding sugar beet and doing all kinds of simple and menial tasks. A tractor and trailer would pick up the volunteers and we would get a meal plus a supply of bread enough to keep the 'family' going. Each bunch of tiny sugar beets had to be thinned out leaving the strongest standing within a few inches of the other; a job best done on your knees since bending down would cripple the most athletic in no time. With padding on the knees it was no great hardship. We also, in due time, collected greenery and loose grain to feed our chickens and thus assured our supply of eggs.

A simple way of getting meat was to locate and catch hamsters. Not the tiny ones that we have as pets, but the larger variety known, apparently, as golden hamsters that lived in the cornfields and were as much of a pest to farmers as are rabbits. You found a patch of corn which was obviously being nibbled. Having found all the entrances you blocked off all but two of them. By putting smoking straw down one hole you were more or less sure of a hamster emerging coughing and sneezing through the remaining hole. All that was needed was an accurate thump on his head and you had as much meat as you would get from a pigeon or very small chicken. It even tasted like chicken. The bonus of such a kill was also the supply of undigested grain these busy little creatures kept in their cheek pouches. This we then fed to the chickens.

The railway sidings were a bit of a problem. Great during the day for kids to play on - in spite of, or perhaps because of - being off limits and causing railway guards to chase us and threaten dire punishments. At night, however, it seemed obvious that sooner or later the railway would be bombed and even if this were to be done with pin-point accuracy, the chances of the houses surviving seemed slim. To add to this natural worry, every night without fail, around about 9.00 p.m., some genius in a plane arrived and lit up the whole countryside with flares. These were soon zoomed in on by whole squadrons of heavy bombers which circled about for a bit and then set off in various directions. They never did bomb the sidings but no one thought to tell us that the flares were a regular way of making sure that the raiding bombers from all over Britain would meet and be accurately re-directed towards their targets. Allied air supremacy was practically absolute by then but even so the task of marking this spot night after night was a highly dangerous business. It was only many years later (while I was at the seminary) that I actually met the man - Group Captain Leonard Cheshire - who led the Pathfinders and earned his Victoria Cross by repeatedly and regularly flying a fast but unarmed Spitfire deep into enemy territory (our back garden, in fact) to drop these markers. He duly apologised for my sleepless nights.

Not knowing any of this and feeling like pimples on a pudding in such bright illumination, most of the populace used to pack their essential belongings every night, take a few blankets and camp out a half mile or so away in the dry bed of a small river. This gave not only some distance but also some shelter from what everyone expected, every night, would be a bombing raid destroying the sidings and sheds plus the small town with it. After three or four hours of such Blackpool illuminations no more flares were put down, all the heavy stuff droned off into the distance and we cheerfully and gratefully returned to our beds. A few more hours and we heard the much lighter tones of returning planes passing directly overhead without having to pause and re-orientate themselves and going back home to their bacon and egg breakfasts - which, again, is only something I read about much later was the modest reward to the air crews for their night of risking their lives.

In the daylight hours the sky was filled with American planes going over high overhead to their bombing targets - probably Berlin. They looked like silver toys in the sunlight and were escorted by fighters even though the opposition, as far as we could see, was non-existent. The road passing through Gusten was quite a major highway for those days. It was dead straight and lined with cherry trees. The fruit did not seem to be the property of anyone in particular but the grass verges were never wasted. They were let to individuals who either fed their chained goat on their patch or harvested the grass for hay. This highway was regularly machine gunned if anything interesting was seen moving on it. I remember standing on the wall of a dry well watching idly as the planes went by when suddenly a fighter seemed to come straight out of the sun aiming at me personally. Without hesitation I dived down the well, only some six feet deep and filled with rubbish, and when I was eventually rescued and my stupidity at rubbernecking was pointed out forcefully we also found a line of chips which the bullets had neatly carved all along the wall I had been so cheerfully using as a vantage point. What with general bombings and Dresden and now this it was being suggested more and more that perhaps I was either destined for higher things or being reserved for the gallows.

It was obvious even to the innocent, unpolitical and news starved populace mainly concerned with their own survival that the war was rapidly coming to an end. Military transport used the road at night in a haphazard fashion in either direction with little apparent organisation or purpose; once a long line of men and women wearing what seemed like pyjamas were driven through the town, on foot, with guards and dogs while we kids looked with utter horror and equal lack of understanding but an uncanny fear and dread. We were waved off by the guards, forbidden to stand and stare and told that these were 'bad people' from what were known as special camps; and then the subject was dropped.

It is difficult to believe in this day and age of universal 'news' and when faced with documented and pictorial proof of what went on in these concentration camps that the people of Germany did not know about it. Many did; some in great detail; they must have done. But for most ordinary people there were rumours and stories which were so outrageous that they were incredible. They were thought to be grossly exaggerated; there was a constant and concentrated propaganda on radio and in the papers that demoralising lies were being spread by the enemy. There was a ten year history of brainwashing that there was 'an enemy within' consisting of Jews, gypsies, slavs, homosexuals, inadequates and criminals who had to be segregated because they were a danger to the state. There was a lot of fear, a lot of uncertainty, a tremendous distrust of one's neighbour who might or might not denounce one to the authorities. There was the daily effort to look after one's own, keep your nose clean, don't get involved. None of this and many other factors are an excuse; just a partial explanation. But it is just one more proof of the saying that ' the first casualty of war is truth'.

By now, of course, there was the overriding anxiety as to what was about to happen, what the end of the war would bring. Much more effort was put into the daily search for food, to stock up for an uncertain future, to gather whatever was going just in case it would come in useful. This, in our area, consisted mostly of raiding the goods wagons which were simply standing around in the sidings, unguarded and going nowhere. Civilised organisation was breaking down. One week we would manage to get whole bales of camouflage material so that all our clothing was made out of it by the local mothers. Trousers, shirts and jackets were a bit stiff but virtually indestructible; next it would be piles of grey army blankets; ideal for overcoats, curtains and black-out sheets. Then there were bales of brilliant white parachute silk perfect for girl's blouses and skirts. [Years later when at school in Buckingham I still had a pair of football shorts made of this material and discovered, when playing on a rainy afternoon, to my embarrassment and general amusement, that the material became transparent when wet!] Even more exciting was the discovery of a wagon or so of sausages and bacon, even though this was not my favourite food. There was even a great trade in horsemeat so that when a poor old nag had to be put down the local town crier, ringing his bell, would go around advertising a sale and we would all queue up for our rations. I used to barter my bits for butter and cheese whenever possible. Chocolates, sweets and exotic fruits were quite unknown but there was always home-made toffee based on sugar beet and other tit-bits which the local population at all times and in all circumstances managed to provide somehow for birthdays or other festive occasions.

The war did end; bit by bit as the occupying forces reached various parts of Germany. The Americans entered Gusten; gently and gingerly. Except in large cities or the actual fighting front, each village or small town was approached by a spearhead consisting of a suicidal Yank in a jeep followed closely by some tanks and under an umbrella of fighters and bombers. If there was no resistance, the troops fanned out, searched the area, left some troops to keep an eye on the place and continued to the next settlement. If there was resistance then the jeep reversed at great speed, the tanks stopped and opened fire and the planes flattened all opposition without discriminating between military or civilian areas. Word soon got around that the best thing to do was simply to sit tight, not allow fanatics to fight any rearguard and futile action and allow oneself to be peacefully occupied. This we cheerfully did in Gusten. Rumour had it that there was a 'hero' in the town who wanted to set up a machine gun and fight. Somehow he was said to have been neutralised and soon an unnatural calm fell on the district; a strange atmosphere of expectation; no traffic, no planes, no activity anywhere. A jeep appeared in the distance on the road passing our house into the town, crossed the bridge over the dry river very carefully and stopped. A number of planes circled overhead, we kids all ran out to see the action and the jeep was followed by some tanks and lorries with men in strange uniforms grinning warily and throwing us what turned out to be chewing gum. In no time the planes dispersed, the Americans searched the houses and visibly started to relax and we had been occupied. It was as simple as that. The war had ended - for us.

Practically next day my mother found a German speaking American and explained our situation, nationality and desire to get in touch with Sweden. This was soon done by a letter through the army post office and we sat back to await results. The town was peaceful, no more bomber formations overhead at night, the Americans were simply accepted and took over the local government, the distribution of food, the gradual restoration of transport and general order. The wagons in the sidings were even easier to get at now and we continued to scavenge whenever possible and whatever it happened to be; immediately useful or not, which is where one more deliverance from my possible death comes in.

I had a bad cold and was barred from roaming around with the usual crowd of youngsters for a day or so. They had discovered an ammunition wagon - no less. Pinching shells and bullets they apparently had this brilliant idea of taking out the gunpowder and heaping it into a nice pile in order to light it. I was watching from my bedroom window when some genius applied the match and the whole thing went off with disastrous results. One lad died of his burns and several others suffered various degrees of injury. It was a horrific sight of kids running and screaming and rolling in the dust to put out their burning clothing. There but for the grace of God and the flu germ I would surely have been as well; possibly with dire results. Instead, we had a case of what the experts described as apparently spontaneous combustion. The ammunitions train in the sidings had a wagon loaded with landmines. For reasons never really discovered this caught fire one Sunday lunch time and the first anyone knew was a tremendous explosion which rocked the whole of the house. A section of a wagon with a buffer still attached landed in the garden and most of the windows shattered. On rushing outside the source of the explosion was obvious - a huge cloud of smoke along the railway with continuing flashes and explosions of small arms ammunition and, obviously, the risk that another wagon of heavy stuff would go up spectacularly. Most people retired again to the dry river bed while the Americans used a tank to unhitch the rest of the train and make things safe. Rumour had it that several soldiers were injured and it was a bit of a miracle that nobody along our row of houses suffered injury and that the damage was frightening but minimal.

The war was officially over in Europe and in due time a letter arrived from Sweden; delivered triumphantly by a little Yank who spoke fluent German. The senior aunt nun - the one real sister of my father - wrote that dad was alive and well and had been in that happy state in England since the middle of 1940. This was the first time we had received an uncensored letter giving us this news. Furthermore, she had informed him of our survival and our present position and he was on his way over to meet and collect us. "*Stay put*" she wrote and details of his arrival were to follow. Unfortunately, the other bit of news the American had was that due to an agreement reached long before at a summit conference between Churchill, Stalin and Roosevelt the zones of occupation in Germany had been fixed even before the invasion of the continent and were to be put into practice no matter where the actual troops came to rest at the end of hostilities. Our bit now belonged to the Russians. The Americans were to withdraw forthwith and the Russian allies would take over.

The war was officially over in Europe and in due time a letter arrived from Sweden; delivered triumphantly by a little Yank who spoke fluent German. The senior aunt nun - the one real sister of my father - wrote that dad was alive and well and had been in that happy state in England since the middle of 1940. This was the first time we had received an uncensored letter giving us this news. Furthermore, she had informed him of our survival and our present position and he was on his way over to meet and collect us. "*Stay put*" she wrote and details of his arrival were to follow. Unfortunately, the other bit of news the American had was that due to an agreement reached long before at a summit conference between Churchill, Stalin and Roosevelt the zones of occupation in Germany had been fixed even before the invasion of the continent and were to be put into practice no matter where the actual troops came to rest at the end of hostilities. Our bit now belonged to the Russians. The Americans were to withdraw forthwith and the Russian allies would take over.

This news was greeted with consternation by the natives and not least by ourselves. We had battled our way 'west' all these months only to be overtaken by the dreaded Russkies. The Americans were bidden a tearful farewell, gave us kids our final chewing gum and sweets and withdrew in good order; back over the little bridge and off to their demarcation lines established by the powers that be at the Yalta or some other conference long ago. Within a matter of hours the Russians came into Gusten from the other end of the town to a reception so markedly different that even the memory of it remains bizarre.

Word had spread on the bush telegraph that as the Russians came into a town or village - not the seasoned and disciplined fighting troops from the front line but raw conscripts and second rate divisions - the best way to welcome them was by hanging out red flags from your front windows and then lying low in your cellar until they settled in. The whole place erupted with red flags with the more zealous and imaginative inhabitants hastily stitching on a white hammer and sickle. We peered out warily at the procession of tractors and old lorries and even horse drawn vehicles (with the distinctive Russian harness of a large hoop over the horse's shoulders) straggling into town and deploying round the area. No smart jeeps, no tanks, no lorries with friendly soldiers throwing chewing gum. This lot were scruffy and perched on top of their baggage and provisions. Some jumped down if they saw anyone on the road and promptly confiscated watches and wallets and anything else that might look valuable. It was not uncommon to see a soldier with a collection of watches proudly strapped from wrist to elbow. All houses were searched once again but this time with brutality and as much damage to doors and furniture as possible; Just a rabble breaking into each home and with much hoarse yelling and shouting and intimidation plundering whatever they could manage to carry away with them. There were widespread reports of rape and pillage and devastation and brutal retaliation if there was a hint of opposition. The whole experience lasted a few hours and was quite terrifying; if only because it was such a contrast to the civilised and orderly American entry just a few weeks before.

Things calmed down again but there was an atmosphere of deep fear and suspicion. However, they were, after all, our allies. The Americans had told my mother as much and that she should get in touch with the local H.Q. and tell them about Sweden and the plans for my father coming in the very near future to collect us. Some Russian dialects are very much like Polish and, with some effort, a simple conversation can be conducted. She duly reported herself and stated our case. Only to be told that all Poles were now the subjects of the Russians and that we as a family would be taken 'home' the very next day. As to this character who had been in England all through the war, he was no better than a traitor to the Polish cause and would certainly not be allowed to come near us. In a state of considerable shock my mother went to ask the advice of the Parish Priest (who had been instructing me, now for the second time in my young life and this time in German, for First Holy Communion). He seemed to have some inside knowledge of events and was not surprised that we were going to be 'taken home' pronto. His advice was to leave quietly, there and then, and get lost in the migration of souls going on at that time when people were travelling in all directions trying to get home from wherever the end of the war had trapped them. He suggested we should try and get to Berlin which was a jointly occupied city and where there was more possibility of making contact with the British and Americans. He quickly arranged for a parishioner to give us a rail permit and we boarded a train next day at crack of dawn going vaguely in the direction of Berlin. There were no time tables nor any organised system of transport. We only got as far as Magdeburg, still under the Russians, before the train was shunted into a siding and the best bet was to start walking - with many others - in, we hoped, the right direction. It was also at this point that my older sister, by then twenty, insisted on returning to Poland, much against my mother's wishes as well as common sense. From then onwards her life took a very different route and we have not met since. All this was August/September 1945.

We learned much later that the good couple who had welcomed us and shared their house with us were, in fact, visited next day and had some nasty moments when it was discovered that these Polish birds had flown. Fortunately, the whole country was in such chaos, there were all kinds of Eastern Europeans and other even more shady characters fleeing in various directions, that our hosts did not suffer any more grievous harm than a few days of great fear and anxiety in the expectation of reprisals. Apparently the parish priest was suspected but with the luck and the usual expertise of the clergy and due to the general disorder prevailing at the time nothing was actually made to stick and he survived unscathed. The Russians had far greater and more important things to worry about than just one family. For all this we have remained duly grateful but with discretion being the better part of valour we were also advised not to renew or prolong contact with the couple who, with no other alternative, had to remain in what became known as the Russian Zone and, eventually, East Germany. They do, however, deserve our gratitude and praise for their generosity in putting us up in our time of need; irrespective of nationality and all because of a fleeting meeting at the graveside of their son. [We did get in touch when we eventually reached England and I remember my father insisting on even sending a parcel of goodies to start showing his gratitude. But the response was a veiled plea not to rock the boat; dictators and tyrants have long memories and correspondence with the West at that period of the cold war was not healthy. Those who never experienced this, including Dad, never really understood the fear, uncertainty, suspicion and sheer terror which were the tools of the trade keeping such regimes in being.]

As we made our way, with lots of other refugees or what became known as 'DP's' - displaced persons - in the direction of Berlin partly by odd lifts in carts or lorries, partly in goods trains but mainly on foot; sleeping on railway stations or wherever there was some shelter, my father was on his way from England. He had been given compassionate leave from Halton camp where he was an instructor in the R.A.F. and found a spot on one of the many planes going to Germany with troops and provisions. His story of going off to meet his long lost family evoked great sympathy and practical help until he reached the frontier between East and West Germany. There the Americans made it quite clear that there was no way he could enter the Russian zone. They may all have been technically allies but the Russians would not welcome someone in British uniform with Polish nationality into their zone. He was left in no doubt that if he did enter he would have little chance of returning - with or without his family - and neither the Americans nor the British would be able or willing to lift a finger to help him. He regarded all this as sheer propaganda and argued, in his political simplicity, that surely the Russians would not do this to their allies - as both the British and the Poles were still generally and officially considered to be. He carried on to the frontier and somehow, possibly in some shady deal, acquired a bicycle on which he was going to complete his journey having swopped his uniform jacket for a neutral looking coat. Fortunately, he was arrested by the French - God knows what they were doing there - and managing to identify himself he was hauled back to rejoin his uniform and be flown back to Halton. Not quite in handcuffs but definitely under a cloud.

No amount of pleading and agitation had any effect in obtaining official permission to go to Germany again. But in a week or so he got more news. Through the Americans in Berlin a letter arrived in my mother's very own hand saying we were now in that city, in a D.P. camp under allied control and could he, please, get over and see to his family etc. Again, he got compassionate leave and the whole story was getting quite romantic and plucking various official heartstrings in Halton. He landed in Berlin and reached the camp in Spandau to be told that yes, this lot had been here for some weeks but we had been transported further to the west into the heart of the British Zone and could be found at yet another camp, Fallersleben.

Changing the scene back to us; we had during this time actually reached Berlin and reported ourselves to an official D.P. camp. We registered, proved our identity and established our credentials as a family with solid prospects of being accepted either in Sweden by saintly aunts or in Britain by a genuine husband and father in the R.A.F. This sort of situation was considered a gilt-edged guarantee that we would be sent on down the line as soon as was convenient. We were sitting pretty in comparison to the majority of individuals and families who were officially 'stateless', with nowhere to go, no one to guarantee a home for them. Canada, America, Australia, Sweden and all kinds of countries were willing to accept D.P.'s but they had to be vetted, join a long waiting list and had no certainty whatsoever of getting there. There are still, sixty years later, stateless people living in Germany either in camps or special housing and waiting for legalities to be completed so that they can find some place officially called 'home'.

The camp was crowded with men, women, children of every nationality under the sun. It was an old army camp, the Americans fed us and we were lucky to have a room per family. People came and went every day, everyone lived in the hope that they could depart as soon as possible to wherever they were hoping to be going. My most vivid memory is the sight of my first black man - in the flesh. He was married, presumably, to a white woman and they had a tiny baby in a pram. It goes some way to show the innocence or ignorance either of that time or my own particular obtuseness that I was desperate to see the baby. I genuinely suspected that it would be either polka dotted or striped! And great was my surprise to see this lovely chocolate coloured bambino. I was ten and a bit by then! Perhaps there are some arguments in favour of sex education in schools after all - if one actually attended school, which I was still gleefully missing.

As historians now know the whole idea of dividing Berlin among the four allies was fraught with problems. To begin with, the city was an island in the Russian Zone and could not be approached from any direction except through their check points. The Russians also claimed a proprietorial right over all nationals of countries they had 'liberated' - the whole of eastern Europe. They insisted that these should be sent back as soon as possible and it was not uncommon for snatch squads to descend on the Berlin camps and take away these individuals and families. Short of a pitched battle there was little a camp commander, British, American or French, could do in such circumstances. Because of this danger and since it had been clearly established that we would have no problem finding a home in England we were soon marked out for transporting into the British zone. The only way to do this was to sneak as many D.P.'s as possible into bona fide military transport going into that zone; either troops going off on leave or exchange or lorries trundling off to fetch provisions and rations. The well known and loved Bedford trucks were used for this and we found our places in the back of one of those and set out. There were frequent stops and hold-ups but even the Russians did not have the cheek to search military transport though they must have suspected that there were civilian 'Russian' nationals on board. In due time, we reached a place called Fallersleben, near Brunswick, which was yet another of the many military/youth/ workers camps left over from the Hitler regime.

This time, however, it was utterly chaotic. There were masses of people milling around and new ones coming in every hour. The buildings were mostly in ruins and no kind of reception procedure had been organised. The trucks simply unloaded their human freight and departed while people tried to find where and how to register, where to find a roof over their heads and where the next loaf of bread could possibly come from. There was no future in staying and we decided to hike out into the countryside and try to find some sort of shelter for that night. A mile or so out we stopped and sat on our suitcases with dusk falling and no sign of a village or habitation in sight. A lone car appeared, rather smart, silver Citroen of the type which would become familiar much later on the T.V. as typical of that famous French detective. [No, not Poirot; he is one of the few famous Belgians; Maigret.] A lone French officer was driving and he slowed down to ask what we were doing and where on earth we thought we were going. In schoolgirl French and much pseudo-Gallic waving of hands my mother managed to explain that we did not have a clue except that the camp we had left behind us offered no solution. The chap seemed to agree, told us to get in and drove off to Brunswick where he delivered us to yet another camp. This one was a model of good order. It was the first time we came across men and women in grey uniform with a green beret whom we later came to know and value and cherish as 'Quakers'. Either through religion or personal conviction they were conscientious objectors who had probably served in the ambulance and medical corps through the war and were now employed in organising camps, sorting out stateless persons, rounding up the thousands of wandering and lost individuals in occupied Germany; irrespective of race, nationality or religion.

In spite of valiant efforts through the years and talking to modern-day Quakers and visiting their prayer rooms [most recently in Bedford] no one seems to have a clear picture of just how many of them were involved and what they did in the years immediately after the war. Their H.Q. in London seems to have no official history or records of these activities and of those who had actually been active then not all that many are still surviving. Considering how much has been written about far smaller units of divers, special services, parachutists, infiltrators, war crimes investigators and others, it seems a pity that the work of these units - conspicuous by their efficiency and gentleness and just being there when most needed - does not appear to have been immortalised.

We got a small room with one bed for the three of us. Regular simple but adequate meals and clothes where necessary. Our arrival was duly recorded and notification sent, through regular channels, to poor old Dad in England. The camp was roughly divided into nationalities and - horror of horrors - the Poles were already running a school for the children. We were duly required to attend this every morning but, again, I can remember nothing except that our knowledge of German was regarded with some suspicion by the good patriots. It was a 'holding camp' with the inmates not guarded nor detained in any way but quite unable to do anything themselves about their future. People were simply waiting for passports, visas, official 'invitations' from countries of their choice or, even for simple transport to take them back from wherever they had fled or been transported.

So we waited while my father was directed from Berlin to Fallersleben where he found, on arrival, that there were hardly any records of anybody and certainly not ourselves. We had only been there an hour or so, a few faces among so many, not been registered nor made any other mark. Nobody knew of the French officer, who had given us a lift, so as far as father or the authorities were concerned we had simply vanished. Camps, transit stations, pockets of refugees were all over the place and his compassionate leave was over in any case. Once more he returned to Halton after a fruitless search. He got in touch with Sweden but they had not heard anything since our stay in Berlin. The trail seemed to have gone cold; even come to a dead end.

It took about three weeks for a letter to reach him giving the address of our new residence. Another week or so for him to get more leave since by then his camp commander was, apparently, beginning to think that this search was a figment of his imagination. Again he managed to get a lift in some transport plane and through Celle - a small town near Hanover which was the staging post for all Air Force personnel going in and out of Germany - he got a lift to the camp and actually found us duly registered and still on the spot.

On returning from this local 'school' at lunch time we found my mother and a man in our room both in tears. My sister, nearly three years older, recognised him at once. I was very dubious and checked with my mother as to who this could be; was it really my father? From his reaction it was obvious that he was and so, at last, we were re-united. He was also appalled at the conditions in which we were living and that very day he took us away to a village called Burgdorf near Hannover. Through the Air Force we were settled at once into a small hotel. He then had to return to England and start the process of getting the necessary entry permits. He left with us a suitcase full of chocolate, sweets and tins of ham, bacon, cheese and Spam. He had been hoarding all this from his rations through the years knowing, of course, through Sweden that we are alive and confident that we would get together again. Some of the chocolate was getting white with age but we had not seen such luxuries for years and it seemed quite reasonable to eat a bar at a time or creep out of bed and open a tin of ham or cheese and scoff it. I stuck mainly to the chocolate and cheese since even then I was not all that desperate for bacon and ham; although quite partial, even now, to the generally derided Spam.

After a few days at the hotel we were moved to the top floor of a large house which belonged to a jam factory owner. It was allocated to us by the British authorities but there was no ill will about it. The owner, a young man with wife and two small children, was quite happy to have us there. We went to the hotel every day for the main meal - paid for with special vouchers - and were otherwise catered for by the R.A.F. with a weekly delivery of food. It was a glorious four or five summer months. I used to go with the truck into Hannover with the airmen most weeks to stock up the base with provisions. A special box was filled for us with unheard of luxuries such as white bread, butter and cheese, chocolate, coffee and tea and I used to drink a tin of condensed milk at a sitting without a second thought. Cigarettes were the currency at the time and with these supplied as well we could buy more or less anything we wanted. The house was next to a wood where I roamed with the so-called guard dog from the factory next to the house. All they produced at the time was a kind of thick, black syrup made from sugar beet and I was great pals with the caretaker/chief mechanic and his wife who had lost their one and only son in the war. As a side-line the few workers there also made scooters (the ordinary, old fashioned ones) and I was given one to run about on through the village. I fashioned a front brake for it but nobody thought to tell me that if you slam on the front brakes on a scooter you fly off into space which I did - with some damage to the head and a badly skinned knee but another experience under my belt; still no school and the ever surer prospect of getting to England coming daily nearer.

When the time came to leave we were quite sorry to go. If only because we were going utterly into the unknown with no language and no idea where we would live and what life would be like. My caretaker friend gave me a small statue of a dog in bronze - which I have treasured since and now passed on into safe keeping in the hope that it will, eventually, become a genuine antique. We set off by train to Calais surrounded by British soldiers going home on leave. It was July 1946 and we were met at Dover by my father who said we were going to some place called Luton. The journey by train through incredibly green fields and towns unscathed by bombing was a trip into a new world. In Germany most big towns were so much in ruins that one could hardly tell where the streets had been, never mind the houses. London itself had, of course, been bombed but was so huge that ruins were just the occasional scars. In comparison to Hannover and other cities the damage seemed negligible. We arrived in Luton to lodge with a couple, some friends of my father's, who had issued the official invitation to us to come to England and given the necessary assurance that we would have somewhere to live.

It was a semi-detached house on what was then the very outskirts of Luton opposite the golf club on the Bedford Road. July and August were exceptionally sunny and hot and I started every day by having a breakfast of corn flakes - brand name of 'Farmer's Glory - with plenty of milk and sugar and then spent the rest of the day across the road roaming around the golf course. It may, again, be fond imagination but what I remember most was the constant song of the skylarks and seeing them high up in the cloudless skies. I used to stumble across partridge nests and scare the living daylights out of the poor birds. With nothing better to do I collected lost golf balls and started a thriving business selling them back to the odd players I came across.

It was not a busy course at that time; things were still very much settling down from the war and to the great dismay of the natives bread rationing (although on a very generous scale) was brought in at that time. It had never been rationed throughout the war and here were the victors having to watch every crumb because of the starvation prevailing in the whole of Europe.

My father on a rare visit home with my sister and a cousin – I'm the good looking one!

My father continued at Halton Camp, near Aylesbury, and came for week-ends. It was a two or three mile walk to church in the middle of Luton but it seemed no effort at the time to go every week. The Mass was, of course, in Latin and thus familiar. But the sermon was not only unintelligible but also frightening with a burly priest yelling and gesticulating. It was, of course, the formidable Canon Dalby who frightened far more people than just me. The couple we were staying with were very kind but did tend to exhibit us as some of the first refugees to have come over to England and it was never intended for us to stay with them very long.

Within about six weeks we moved to the tiny village of Tingrith near Toddington and again took over the top of a house. This time it was an old couple, Albert and Freda and their many cats who lived on the ground floor. We had their three bedrooms upstairs and my mother had to go back to cooking and doing the normal housework. My father got a car - an old Ford 8 reg. number EBH 724 - so he could come over from Halton much more often. I got friendly with the local farmers and remember being in on the miracle of the birth of a calf and generally just wandering around and, most probably, being a real nuisance.

The language, of course, was a problem. My mother remembered a few words from her school days. My father spoke what we thought was perfect and fluent English having been in this country since 1940. But we knew not a word and the big black cloud looming over us was the fact that very soon, early September, we would have to attend the local school. Tingrith did not have one but a special bus collected the few kids to take them into Toddington. We hated it! Now and then we managed to sabotage the alarm clock so that we missed the bus. We tried to slink off the bus on arrival and play truant, but the place was far too small for us to be able to hide and our 'fame' had already spread so that we were marked. They had never seen foreigners in Toddington before and the teachers gave us special treatment and showed us off to visitors. The children used to corner us in the playground and either just look at us, comment on the foreign cut of our clothing or keep on asking us to say a few words in Polish or German. They were not cruel, there was no bullying; just constant and persistent curiosity. Not only had we lost the habit of going to school, not only did we hardly understand what was going on, but school lasted all day! We never got back home until the late afternoon. Schools as we remembered them were only attended in the mornings.

Our first Christmas was at Tingrith with careful explanations that it was not Christmas Eve that mattered but the day itself and also this 'Boxing Day' which, we were told, derived its name from the fact that the boxes of presents were only opened then. No carp and beer soup, which was a blessing, but chicken (no turkey that year) and a solid pudding (with, mysteriously, a coin lurking in it ready to break someone's tooth) and mince pies instead of poppyseed cake. Although we lived dead opposite the church it was explained to us that this was not our church but an English one which we could not attend. Instead, we travelled into Ampthill to what is now the local mortuary to be harangued by another large and loud priest; this time a Dutchman who for years was an institution in that parish. He used to sing the 'Pater Noster' in Latin in a very loud voice and all the way back to Tingrith I used to imitate his performance in what was still a boy-soprano register.

Then the winter set in - the harshest one for many a year. We had moved to the outskirts of Aylesbury by then where we bought a three bedroomed, semi-detached house for the princely sum of £1800.00. My father was a senior Warrant Officer with a salary of some £45.00 per month and this was considered to be a good and steady and well paid job at the time. He had no problems getting a mortgage of £1000.

The winter was a real harsh one for this country and we were surprised at just how unprepared people were for a bad winter. In Poland double glazing was standard and heating came from tiled stoves which not only belted out heat but stored it as well. Mere fireplaces were lovely to look at and cosy to sit by but left the rest of the room freezing. Central heating was a rarity and doors and windows seemed designed to let in draughts. Coal was not easy to get but at least we lived near enough to Halton and the woods in that area so that we gathered lots of sticks and small logs. In comparison to the deadly cold that year on the continent - still mostly in ruins - we were lucky.

Father still had his car and since the petrol rationing was rather strict he adjusted the simple engine so that he could run on a mixture of petrol and paraffin. The exhaust was a bit smoky and the 0 to 60 performance not impressive, to say the least. The engine needed de-coking regularly but it was our pride and joy with him doing the mechanics and myself polishing the body. I still remember my admiration of his mechanical skills and the practically fanatical way in which he kept the engine compartment clean as a whistle. In spite of this he actually taught me to drive and - sitting on pillows to be able to see out - I used to drive it on public roads. Highly illegal; but traffic was very sparse. He had bought the car second hand from Canon McHugh, the parish priest in

Aylesbury with whom he used to play chess occasionally. Old McHugh used to say it would be a safe and happy car because of the many years he had used it to take the Blessed Sacrament to the sick.

I went to the local school in Aylesbury while my sister attended the convent in Tring. The first week or two there with the winter in its full rigour, I slipped on a special ice slide we had made in the playground and broke my leg. I spent the rest of that bitter weather sitting at home in plaster and hobbling out on a home-made crutch to collect the freezing birds I caught in my equally home-made trap. This was a garden sieve carefully propped on a stick attached to a long string leading to the front room. A few crumbs of bread attracted the starving birds, a yank on the string trapped them under the sieve and I then retrieved them to warm them up, feed them and set them free. Some did die of heart failure and shock at being caught but mostly I felt like a proper little St. Francis. The rest of my time I spent reading Polish books from the Halton Camp library and being nagged by my father to read English books or I would never learn the language!

In due time I returned to school with a limp and a permanently weaker left leg so that my football career always suffered from the fact that I could kick well and accurately with my right leg, I could foul most artistically and never gave up on even the hardest of tackles but only ever used my left leg to stand on.

I picked up the language as if by magic so that at the end of the term I was placed 37th in a class of 45. This was probably charity unless the other eight pupils were really thick. Within this year the really spectacular difference was that both my sister and myself were increasingly often correcting poor old dad in his grammar, pronunciation and even his vocabulary. His command of English did turn out to be indeed fluent but very much 'foreign'.

While still in Tingrith and attending Ampthill church I was most impressed by a visiting Mill Hill priest sporting a full black beard and wearing a beautiful red sash round his ample middle. He spoke about the missions to the Eskimos who, as it happened, were my favourite people at the time. I loved to read the stories of polar explorers, Canadian trappers and the Inuit and their lives and customs. I decided that I would become a missionary priest and go there in due time. Since I kept on going on about this and in spite of my father saying that as soon as I got a bit older and met a nice girl I would change my mind, we investigated a bit further and discovered that the first step would have to be attendance at a Catholic school or Junior seminary for the order which happened to be in Liverpool. My vocation cooled rapidly when I realised just how far Aylesbury was from Liverpool. It cooled even further when I kept on reading and hearing that the Inuit lived on fat and blubber - I never could stand fat. Nor was my vocation strengthened on reading in various books on the subject of Eskimos that human urine was commonly stored and used for various purposes including the regular washing of one's hair to give it a silky sheen!

The last blow came when my father mentioned, during one of his games of chess with Canon McHugh, that he had this weird son who was going on about the Mill Hill fathers. The response was very positive and constructive: why go on missions into the unknown when our own Diocese wanted priests. The Bishop was coming shortly and would have a look at me. This was Bishop Leo Parker and he gave me the once-over in the Canon's sitting room and decided that I ought to go to the nearest Catholic school. This was in Buckingham; only some 18 miles away. It was run by Franciscans but in no way exclusively for their own vocations. It was a boarding school where those who had expressed a wish to join the order were educated in a normal manner (for that day and age) together with other Catholic lads from eleven upwards who wanted to be anything or nothing plus a few known as 'Bishop's boys' who were more or less earmarked for the Diocese.

In due course, September 1947, I was taken to Buckingham and left there as a boarder aged 12 getting on for 13 and the first time away from home. It might just as well have been on the moon as far as I was concerned. To my continued shame and utter lack of understanding the reason why, I was incredibly home-sick. In the first three weeks it was so intense that I was practically ill and on the first visit allowed by parents I had to be peeled away from the car as they left to go back to Aylesbury.

The kindly headmaster (known in the order as the Guardian) pointed out that if I did want to be a priest then I ought to remember that Jesus had to leave his parents and go out into the world to preach and that, no doubt, he was homesick and unhappy as well. My rather scathing reply became a classic often quoted in later years: that it was O.K. for Jesus; he was 30 by then and I was still only twelve! Things improved, of course, but unlike almost all of the pupils who returned from their holidays time after time full of the joys of youth I never went back without at least a week or two of utter misery. This continued all through the six years there and even into seminary years. In fact, it even worked the other way round so that when, much later, I went home from a six month stretch at the seminary I was 'home sick' for the seminary! Presumably I must be one of those people who simply lack imagination, get institutionalised very quickly and just do not like change. I would probably make a very good jailbird but hope never have to put this to the test.

The start of my undistinguished academic career coincided with my father being ' demobbed' from the Air Force. In one way or another he had served as an instructor for 20 years or more and was technically quite a genius in metalwork and mathematics. One of his major disappointments continued to be the fact that his one and only son was a moron at any kind of mathematics. He joined a Polish school for engineering apprentices in Lilford, near Oundle - strangely much later to be actually in my parish when in Thrapston. Because the Polish 'branch' of the R.A.F. was only a temporary, wartime, arrangement there was no service pension or even golden handshake. But his salary in Lilford was generous, the prospects for the next few years were good and the only problem was the distance from Aylesbury. Even so, he had the car and travelled home most week-end.

The place had been an army camp and ammunitions depot and consisted of the usual collection of huts with the actual Lilford Hall mothballed since it had ceased being an officers' mess. I went to stay there for two or three days during this first half-term from my school. Father taught engineering and had plenty of room and opportunity to indulge his agricultural leanings by having a vegetable garden and starting a flock of young cockerels. He got about 50 of them, a day old, for a song and planned to feed them up and sell them at Christmas for a huge profit. Unfortunately, they all got some funny disease which crippled their little legs and he had practically to give them away at only seven or eight weeks old and carrying not much more meat than the average pigeon. He was just starting a new venture - ducks - on the theory that the wet weather would not affect them.

The first holiday, Christmas, it was more or less arranged that at the end of my term I would travel to Lilford for a few days and then we would go back together to Aylesbury on December 23rd, picking up my suitcase etc from Buckingham on the way. For some reason I decided to go straight home instead and was there on the 23rd when, late in the evening and well after we had expected my father to have arrived home, the police called to tell us that he had had an accident and 'was seriously injured'. In fact, he had been killed on the spot and the poor young policeman just chickened out of telling us this there and then.

Reflection

O Jesus, Lover of souls, we recommend unto you the souls of your servants, who have departed with the sign of faith and sleep the sleep of peace. We beseech you, Lord our Saviour, that, as in your mercy to them you became man, so now you would admit them to your presence above. Gracious lord, we beseech you, remember not against them the sins of their youth and their ignorance; but be mindful of them in your heavenly glory. May the heavens be opened to them. May the Archangel ST Michael conduct them to you. May your holy Angels come forth to meet them, and carry them to the city of the heavenly Jerusalem. May they rest in peace.

John Henry Newman [blessed]

The designs of car safety have progressed a long way since then. The little Ford 8 built in 1938 was a sturdy car with genuine bumpers and real metal body. The steering wheel, however, was mounted on a solid metal rod which, in a head-on collision, simply drove straight up into the drivers chin and smashed his head into the roof. There was, apparently, hardly any sign of injury on my father but his skull was fatally fractured on impact. The accident happened at around mid-day just opposite the Northampton Crematorium (the original road is now by-passed by a more modern highway) the other driver was slightly injured and my father's passenger - a friend being given a lift to get to London - had a cracked rib and slight facial injuries.

We had been in the country just about 18 months but it is amazing how many friends rallied round to help. Old Canon McHugh of blessed memory organised a taxi to take us to Northampton that night and return us to a very empty home after my mother had identified the body. He phoned Cathedral house and asked the priest there to welcome us and take us to the police station. We arrived quite late at night and the door was opened by this giant of a priest - now known as Canon Jim Galvin - who was a raw curate there at the time. He directed the taxi to the police station where we went through all the necessary formalities and were handed all the contents of the car. We brought back with us four live ducks which were in a sack on the back seat - fit and well and causing havoc in the local police station. [In due time we ate three of them while the fourth lived to a ripe old age as a pet roaming the garden and coming into the house to play with the cat]. Christmas was not a happy feast and Boxing Day would have been the 25th anniversary of my parents' wedding. The funeral had to wait over the holiday but somehow friends dealt with the language problem, the death certificate and funeral arrangements, the legal tangle due to the lack of a will, the paying off of the mortgage with the £1000.00 insurance from the car crash and innumerable other details.

Looking back I cannot but be filled with admiration as to how my mother coped in a strange country, no income (he had been in civil employment less than three months - therefore no widow's pension; nor had there been any Air Force pension) two children to feed and educate plus the obvious personal loss and grief and the irony that after all the effort to get to England and the six years of separation he should now be dead. I personally had really only known him for those 18 months and we were not even allowed, for some bureaucratic or medical reason, to see his body. The only thing I managed to rescue was his ring which the undertakers were proposing to bury with him but I insisted I ought to keep - and still treasure.

The untimely death of my father almost certainly changed the whole course of my life. It is most probable that, had he lived, we would have returned to Poland as soon as the circumstances allowed it. Not in 1948, but by the middle fifties, the attitude of the authorities there was changing. After the war those Poles who were tardy in returning had been declared enemies of the state; their property was confiscated and, if they did return in their own time, their welcome was uncertain. This was the only reason why my father was delaying his return. It is not that he was a great patriot - but he was 'a man of the soil' and longed to return, take over the farm from his very aged father and settle down. Had he lived it is most probable that my education would have been very different and, who knows, I may well have ended up as a farmer (instead of a frustrated keeper of the odd donkey, horse, pig, goat or chicken) and not a priest at all. Fortunately, only God knows the future and 'what would have happened if...' (what theologians call 'contingencies') so we will never know.

My Grand Mother's Grave

My sister was assisted to remain at the convent school and the Bishop got in touch immediately and proposed to pay the fees for my continued stay in Buckingham (even arranging for me to have two shillings and six pence pocket money a week - twelve and a half new pence! I think) and all with no strings attached. There could hardly have been any point in binding a 13 year old to enter into a commitment to become a priest. It was a calculated risk prompted by sheer goodness - whether it was worth it may well be arguable. My mother took in lodgers and did odd jobs, we lived frugally and such things as 'holidays' were unheard of. No amount of argument or appeal to get some sort of widow's pension had any effect (the petition even went as far as Downing Street but the rules of military and civilian employment were water-tight) my sister left school at 16 to start work in the office of the solicitor who had helped us at the time of father's death while I worked every holiday at various jobs (telegram boy for quite a while pedalling furiously out to Stoke Mandeville Hospital several times a day and getting to know Aylesbury like the back of my hand) and being convinced at every return to school that I ought to pack it in and get a job as soon as possible. Somehow, becoming a priest continued to seem a good idea and I continued in Buckingham until I was over 18.

My mother with my sister and me in Windsor Great Park

My six years at St. Bernardine's College in Buckingham were not particularly distinguished. It could well be said that I was 'average' in every sense. In one memorable report one of the priest teachers commented that I *worked hard to achieve mediocrity'*. I did not like school. This was in no way the fault of the school to which I am very grateful for my education. The language problem became rapidly less and I soon became fluent to the extent that it became my 'first' language in every sense. I picked up a weird accent which is still with me since the pupil population was very mixed. There were some foreigners but mostly the lads came from all over Britain with a strong representation from Glasgow and thereabouts. This was the influence of the Franciscan presence there and the Order did regard the College as a sort of 'junior seminary' to which any likely characters from Scotland were sent in the hope they would eventually join the Order. Quite a few did so; certainly a greater percentage than those who were there as so called 'Bishop's Boys' who, like myself, were potentially earmarked for the Diocese. Only two of us actually and eventually got ordained and one went as far as the Diaconate and then decided against it.

Education then and education now has only the name in common. Perhaps I'm biased but I do think that it was far broader and more solid than it is now. Examinations were important but not the only purpose of going through school. Possibly because it was a boarding school and had far fewer distractions we did work a lot harder and did regular and lengthy 'homework'. At times our education was beaten in rather than sticking closely to the original definition that it is a 'drawing out'. The facilities in comparison to even the most underdeveloped school today were minimal. We had the essentials: a blackboard, rows of desks, books and exercise books and basic equipment in the laboratory and carpentry workshop as well as some gym equipment. We had teachers, all of them priests except for an ancient Miss Taylor who taught piano and singing. Amazingly, very few of the priests were actually trained teachers. Most had a degree in their subject. Some obviously had to work hard to keep up with the classes. But all of them were dedicated and wanted to share their knowledge and give the boys a love of their subject. Disruption in class was practically unknown and discipline was strict. But in no way was it brutal and I have no memory of anyone ever being cowed, cruelly treated or - even worse - in any way abused physically or sexually. I myself was formally caned three times in six years - and on one of these occasions I was genuinely innocent. In the light of the manifold accusations levelled nowadays against religious orders and their schools and homes I can honestly say that there was never any hint of any kind of abuse. It may well be argued that I myself was probably an ugly youth and would not have attracted the amorous attention of anyone. But there was never any talk, among the boys, no suspicion, no fear nor worry on the subject. I owe a great debt of gratitude to the Franciscans who taught me and, although in this day and age it would be considered very old fashioned, to the standard of education and training I 'enjoyed' at St. Bernardine's College. Enjoyed may well be the wrong word since I did not really like school - especially boarding school - and would probably have had the same attitude even if taught by Archangels.

Football and tennis were my main outlets with cricket a very poor last since I could neither bat nor bowl and spent all my time idling in the outfield hoping for a catch and usually dropping it. I eventually became the official scorer for the first team - mainly because it meant having a posh tea when entertaining another team and going off to visit other schools or clubs. In football I got my 'colours' early on and was notorious for only playing right back, marking the opposing left winger (preferably for life!) and never giving up.

In tennis my style was distinctive and horrible to watch since due to lack of coaching I tended to hold the racket like a club and somehow served and returned the ball low, viciously, accurately and with some sort of top spin which prevented it from bouncing. The whole thing remained a mystery but I managed to win most games. Walking was compulsory, as was cross country running, but with some practice I managed to do as little of both as possible.

Academically I was a dead loss at any sort of mathematics or science and soon gave up both on the grounds that if I did become a priest then profound knowledge of these subjects would be pointless. English, History and Latin were my favourite

Subjects, with French a necessary evil and Greek being utterly ruined because the reverend teacher imagined that it could be whacked into his pupils. The rule was that for every mistake made in a translation we got one stroke from a gnarled old stick on the palm of the hand. The result in my case was that every class was spent sitting on my hands in acute agony and actually never getting beyond the alphabet.

Examinations were not collected as they are now. You either passed the equivalent of 'O' levels or not and took 'A' levels in subjects that would prove useful in your future proposed life. And everyone had quite strong convictions as to what they wanted to do with their life. Not everyone by any means achieved their ambitions but by the age of 14 or 15 it would have been unheard of to say that "I don't know what I want to be". So we specialised. I took my three favourite subjects at 'A' level and passed them; mainly because (apart from another lad who was doing science) I was the only one in the Sixth Form and I was assured by the Bishop that no particular examinations were needed for the seminary! A general education would do and he would decide whether a man was educated or not! This took all the pressure off study and I sailed through the two years in the Sixth treating my subjects as a hobby, reading a vast amount, writing the odd essay, getting a 'tutorial' once a week or so and playing lots of billiards and snooker during class time. This was possible because our Sixth form class room was actually in the billiard room which was itself out on a wing so that the clacking of balls was never too obvious to everyone else on the premises.

Being by this time aged 18 rising 19 and having spent six years as a boarder I left school with no great regrets and still wanting to be a priest. Not 'determined' to be one no matter what; it simply did not occur to me to become anything else. This continued to be a source of wonder to many people. I was not particularly noted for being holy or industrious, pious, gentle or filled with enthusiasm to convert the world. 'Average' would have been an accurate description. Family and friends kept on asking what I was going to do next. Others, such as workmates in the soup factory, Post Office or Income Tax office where I used to work through the holidays to earn enough money to keep going, simply could not understand why I cheerfully announced that I was going to study for the priesthood. An old boy at Nestles factory, been there 25 years mixing soup and slightly deaf, asked me what I was going to college for. When I told him "The priesthood" he replied "Policeman? They'll never have you. You're a short....!" It took him days to get over the surprise that this skinny little fellow mixing soup had such strange aspirations and that the priesthood did not have height standards.

Chapter II

1953-1959 A Priestly Journey

Father Stan, as a young (very) young ordained priest

On the 23rd of May 1959 the Bishop of Southwark ordained nine young men at Wonersh in a long ceremony - all in Latin, lasting nearly four hours and prefaced by the solemn admonition (also in Latin) that anyone leaving during the ceremony for any cause whatever would be excommunicated! The culmination of six years of very full-time study at the seminary and a launching forth into the parishes up and down the country of fresh curates to face a life which in this new century few would believe possible and even fewer would accept as tolerable.

Parish Priest and his two curates in Corby. 1960

I was one of these young men and the life and experience in the seminary and out in the parish as a curate was not, in most ways, extraordinary for the time. It was accepted, it was customary, it even helped to form and train men for the future and was not a life of misery and unhappiness.

It is essential to remember that the world was very different. The 'permissive sixties' had not yet dawned, the Beatles had not been invented and the Second Vatican Council was but an idea eternally enshrined in the Holy Spirit and shortly to be infused into the mind of Pope John XXIII who himself had only been enthroned five or six months. Vocations to the priesthood were plentiful enough to enable Bishops to be able to foresee the future with some confidence and learning, study, formation of the individual, was generally done by listening rather than the use of visual aids, electronic gadgets or virtual reality experience.

In the Diocese of Northampton few men were considered for seminary training if they were over the age of 22 or 23. Many went straight from school or, even more horrific, junior seminaries into whatever senior seminary had space to take them. Not having a seminary of our own, Diocesan candidates were sent mainly to Oscott near Birmingham. Others found their way to Rome, Spain, Ware, Upholland or Ushaw in the north or - just a few - to Wonersh near Guildford which served the Diocese of Southwark and allowed spaces to be filled from Brentwood, Nottingham or Northampton; in that order of priority. It was only partly jocularly known as a seminary for gentlemen who allowed a few scruffs to enter to make up the numbers. It was also, reputedly, one of the more strict establishments which made Oscott look like a holiday camp where the only rule was, so it was said, not to light one's pipe from the sanctuary light! It was also based on the very French and puritanical spirituality of St. Sulpice so that students were still half expecting to be taught to tuck in their shirt with a knife and fork and there was an unhealthy and irritating fear that any friendship would inevitably teeter on the verge of being 'particular' - a pseudonym for homosexual. In fact, nothing was further from the mind of students and there was never any shadow of scandal in that respect.

The pecking order having been established according to the source of one's education and the diocese for which a student was destined, it then affected the whole of the six years of a student's existence. The year list started with those who had been to the local junior seminary of Mark Cross and continued with those who were to be ordained for Southwark (the sub-division into Arundel and Brighton had not taken place). Next came those for Brentwood followed by those for Nottingham. Northampton came last unless there was some poor sinner for Gibraltar or some other genuinely foreign diocese. Seating in chapel and refectory, choice of available rooms, calling of attendance rota at the start of the year, reading out examination results, the circulation of lists for bath times and preferences of relaxation in the afternoons (gardening, woodwork, jogging, sports, work in the printing and binding shop etc), even the pick of seating in chapel for relatives at ordinations of minor and major orders - all depended on this hierarchy cast in stone by the original list. The effect may not have been particularly far reaching and traumatic, but the system did have some psychological effect even if it also helped the smooth running of the whole establishment.

I was two from the bottom on the 1953 year list of 23. Of the 13 eventually ordained in 1959 a Nottingham student was ordained in his diocese, a Gibraltarian brought up the rear and eventually got ordained back at home (and is now the Bishop of Gibraltar) and two went back to their home parishes in Ireland, which left me as the last of nine having the Bishop lay his hands upon me and making me *'a priest for ever according to the order of Melchisedech'*- and forgetting to change the Latin formula of swearing obedience to him and his successors. The result being that, technically, I owe no obedience to the Bishop of Northampton! A detail I did not mention to our then Bishop Leo but have reported to bishops ever since with very little apparent concern on their part.

The purpose of these memoirs is not to lament the past or complain of one's lot. Rather to show to the modern generation of priests - and anyone else who might be interested - how things have changed and let them judge whether this has been for good or bad. It is not that students and priests were better then nor that we were in any way hard done by. It was a different world; things were accepted then which now would be considered outrageous in any walk of life. One's expectations were different but one's acceptance and even happiness and contentment were on a par with the expectations. No doubt the training and manner of study, the whole system in seminary, parish and diocese have had an effect on a priest of that vintage and may help to explain - perhaps even partly excuse - the man that is now. Just as reading a personal account of a seaman who served 'before the mast' in Nelson's time and even a century or so ago fills us with wonder and even some horror but gives us a valuable history lesson, so some insight into a system which did not change for many years but has now changed beyond all recognition can give modern man and even woman (!) some idea of the speed and degree of that change. The experiences of a priest ordained let's say in 1935 and one ordained 25 years later are very much the same; differing only in details of transport, the cost of living and various other aspects of life in general. But all that a priest ordained in the year 2000 seems to share with a crumblie of the 1959 vintage is the grace of the sacrament.

Having, therefore, at the tender age of 12 or 13 expressed the wish to become a priest I was provisionally accepted by Bishop Leo Parker for the diocese and went to the Franciscan boarding school at Buckingham as a 'Bishop's Boy' in contrast to those who were earmarked for the Franciscans or the vast majority who were simply there because it was a Catholic school and their ambition was to become a baker, a candlestick maker, doctor, chemist or educated safe-cracker.

All were taught and treated in exactly the same way but the difference from today was that all did want to become something, even if few achieved it. If asked in public they expressed their various and individual and budding ambitions and some even put their hands up to wanting to become priests. The later stages of their education were affected by their choice of a career so that some did Chemistry and Science while others specialised in English and Latin and what would now be called 'humanities'. Most did as little work as possible according to the immutable nature of school boys and all were equally well or badly behaved and caught and punished according to the practices at that time. It was not a junior seminary and no special treatment was given to those who were thinking of the priesthood. In fact, there was a healthy scepticism that they probably would change their minds at the appearance of the first attractive 'chick', as young ladies were then called, or the prospect of some different career.

Leaving school at very nearly the age of 19 I was still considering going on for the priesthood and left my future in the Bishop's capable hands while I did my normal holiday stint of working for the princely sum of 1 shilling and six pence an hour (7 Â½ new pence) in the Nestles soup factory. By the end of August 1953 it began to dawn on me that either the Bishop had forgotten me or the decision had been made somewhere in a smoke-filled Episcopal palace that I had no vocation after all.

The definition of a vocation - then, as now - is not what a chap wants to do or feels that a mysterious voice is telling him to do. It is the calling or acceptance by a bishop or a religious superior. This calling seemed to be lacking by that time but on gently agitating the bishop's secretary (through a supportive Parish Priest) it was cheerfully made known to me in a short note from the Bishop's House - on September 4th - that my presence would be required on September 8th at Wonersh. The letter also added that I would need to have a cassock, a clerical collar, a black suit and six towels. I had the towels, Wonersh was located on the map after some difficulty as being in Surrey, a Green Line coach would get me there via London and the clerical garb would just have to follow in due time.

Clutching my hard-earned wages from the holiday job I set out with a suitcase containing the towels plus other obvious necessities but dressed in grey flannels and blue blazer with a white shirt and a funereal black tie as the only concession to clerical fashion. Being rather fortunate to meet a young man in a dog collar - a genuine 'cleric' starting his fourth year - on the last stages of the coach trip I at least was guided on to a local bus and found the seminary in his company.

Surprisingly, my name appeared on a typed list of new entrants posted at the main door; but inserted in ink before a certain Caruana C. who is the Gibraltarian mentioned above and thus remained on the bottom of that list for the next six years. A room number - which turned out to be a cubicle with a door but walls not reaching the ceiling - in the high 90's was eventually found to be on the third floor and became 'home' for the next year. It had a bed, a chair and small table, a chest of drawers and a lamp. 6.30 p.m. having been mentioned on the list downstairs as being the time for being in the assembly room I followed the general drift of students and was directed by some of my elders and betters to a front bench - with some misgivings from my guides since I was the only one present not wearing a cassock and clerical collar but glaringly obvious in the equivalent of Bermuda shorts - light grey trousers etc as described above.

A short and tubby but very venerable gentleman entered the hall wearing a red-trimmed cassock and purple bellyband followed by an assortment of priests of all shapes and sizes and mostly advanced ages. Everyone stood solemnly to receive the Rector and staff. With no greeting nor introduction the Rector proceeded to call the names of some hundred or so students all preceded by the title of 'Mr.' If present there was a clear reply of 'adsum' which even this civilian knew was the Latin for 'I am present'. The occasional name not bringing forth this reply meant that either someone had changed their mind and not returned or illness or travel delay (neither of them advisable) occasioned their absence. It was a tradition that if someone had decided not to continue their studies after the holidays (or been advised not to do so or even been excluded for some misdemeanour) the name would still be announced and their absence marked by a hollow silence.

A 'Mr. Capstick' was eventually called out in the list of newcomers and with no response forthcoming the Rector looked up, gave the required time for an answer and was still fixing the front bench with a far from benevolent eye when he called my name, received an answer and also noticed the unorthodox garb which nearly, but not quite, put him off finishing the list with 'Mr. Caruana'. [The Mr. Capstick appeared on the list and was duly called for the next two years but nobody actually ever found out who he was or why he was not there.]

The venerable Rector nobly rose above the distraction caused by my sartorial aberration to read - as was done every year - a long Papal instruction on the nature of a vocation and the duties and responsibilities of a seminary student. For the benefit of the newcomers it was then announced that supper would be followed by Night Prayers and the '*Magnum Silentium*' until 6.00 a.m. next morning. Fortunately, talking was allowed during supper so all kinds of helpful tips were asked for and received from either more senior students or those who had already been to the local junior seminary, were near the head of the immutable year list and were immersed in the folklore and practice of a seminary.

After Night Prayers it was an offence punishable with expulsion to talk to anyone except oneself or God (and then only silently) unless dire need or charity required it. Both the need and the charity would only be considered and judged by the Rector in the very unlikely event that either should arise. An exception was made that very night by the Rector pouncing on this quaintly dressed character and, having been shown the letter from Bishop's House giving me all of five days to obtain a wardrobe, he decided that this constituted a lawful excuse to speak. He then summoned a similarly vertically challenged but more senior student and ordered him to lend me his second best cassock and collar. The result was that next morning I was at least properly dressed for 6.30 a.m. church parade.

The system required that one unfortunate student, in the second year, be appointed to be bell ringer for a whole year. All spent their first year dreading getting the job. At 6.00 a.m. every morning, weekdays or Sundays, it was his solemn duty to go up and down every corridor on every floor and energetically ring a handbell to wake people up. Still in the total silence imposed from the end of prayers the night before the keen students burst forth from their rooms to wash and shave and be down in chapel within minutes. The rest of the student body emerged in various states of wakefulness to do the same in due time so that by 6.30 a.m. everyone had to be conscious, washed, shaved, dressed in full cassock and in their rightful place in chapel to start a half hour of meditation or mental prayer.

This exercise is not easy at the best of times but is even more difficult at crack of dawn when sitting down for any length of time can too easily lead to continuing one's slumbers. This did sometimes happen and a charitable neighbour would dig a sharp elbow into the ribs of a nodding meditator to prevent a snore or, even worse, total collapse. Less charitable but more righteous and conscientious characters just ignored the plight of a sleeper and let him take the consequences.

At 7.00 a.m., promptly, the Rector said a final prayer and a general movement of priests and students marked the beginning of Mass. One Mass was said at the high altar for the students in general. Other Masses were said by every priest on the staff at side altars with their designated servers, all, of course at that time, in Latin. On festival days - not high holydays but feasts of some importance - the Mass was sung; amazingly well by the cantors but notably badly (in comparison to Sunday High Mass at a more civilised hour) by the rest. Mass was followed by a brief time of thanksgiving and a silent trooping into the refectory for breakfast. In Advent and Lent this silence continued through breakfast itself but for the rest of the year the period of silence was lifted at that point.

The food was good enough. Institutional, predictable no doubt, but sufficient and with a reasonable choice so that one could have coffee rather than tea and cornflakes rather than porridge. Breakfast was also an informal meal which one could start and end according to one's speed of eating. Quite an important factor, this, since immediately after breakfast one was allowed to smoke!

This smoking rule was one of those set up as a test; an artificial law to shape one's character and to be obeyed for its own sake. A duly registered smoker was allowed to smoke three times a day at certain periods and in designated places. Nobody had to smoke; but a non-registered smoker could not smoke. The times were for half an hour after breakfast, lunch and supper. The places were outside (if not dark) in the common rooms or lavatories. Infringement of any of these details brought about instant dismissal from the seminary on being found out. No appeal, no warning, no extenuating circumstances or diminished responsibility. It was not all that uncommon to lose a student apparently good in all other spheres but overcome by the nicotine habit or just criminally careless about time and place. The first his colleagues were aware of was a vacant place in chapel or refectory or the sight of a fellow trudging down the drive with his suitcase to catch a bus to Guildford and the evil world beyond.

The reason for this rule was in no way directed at the evil of smoking. At that time the risk to health was hardly ever mentioned and non-smokers cheerfully inhaled the polluted air in common rooms, cinemas, theatres, railway compartments as well as in their own homes. The rule was a test case, completely artificial and based on the premise that if a student could not keep such a simple rule which involved no moral decrepitude or infringement of the Decalogue then how could he be expected to keep the commandments and rules and way of life of a future priest. Some may now think this brutal, simplistic and even counter-productive; and they may be right. At the time we all accepted the rules, accepted some as being pointless in themselves but a test worth trying to live up to for the sake of the end we desired. Many students at that time were more advanced in years, some coming in from the Forces and even having given up years of a worthy and successful career. We younger ones admired their obedience and the added difficulty they had in doing this. Smokers simply had to adapt and live in the hope that on most Sundays there would be an extension of smoking after supper if one attended a gramophone concert or lecture or educational film show in the common room. Many a nicotine addict acquired a love of classical music - and often for life - by chain-smoking through two hours or more of such a concert.

I registered as a smoker on my first Christmas Day in the Seminary; 1953. A Capstan full strength cigarette lasted me for the whole two days of Christmas - one or two puffs at a time - while helping to be a scene shifter at the customary Christmas concert. I then became a pipe smoker and kept to the rules until the Christmas of 1957 when I spectacularly broke this law but was never found out! The advantage of a pipe was that it could, and did, serve as a dummy since sucking an empty one during the hours of study could not be construed as smoking and yet gave one a certain simple and pathetic satisfaction. By Christmas 1957 I was a sub-Deacon and head sacristan and after the midnight Mass, having locked up the church and prepared everything for the next morning I decided that nothing drastic could be done to me at that stage even if caught smoking. I went up into the bell tower and admired the moonlit night while smoking a whole pipe with everyone safely tucked up in bed and myself at great risk of frostbite. I did not have any sense of guilt about it but suspected next day that someone, somehow, somewhere would discover my dark secret. Presumably nobody did and so this is my first public confession of this dastardly deed.

Lectures started at 9.00 am and each lasted for 45 minutes. The first two years were set aside for Philosophy but shared with the older students for Scripture and Church History. We sat in serried ranks on hard benches and listened non-stop and as attentively as human nature would allow, making notes, to a professor going on about Aristotle and Plato, the purpose of philosophy in all its branches and the impossibility of studying Theology later on - or even think cogently - without a deep grounding in this science. Students did not ask questions. They listened, they took notes, they then consulted text books and/or original writings in the long periods of private study every night of the week. They did not write essays nor formally have any discussions unless they chose to do so with their fellow students on walks or while having their cherished smokes in times of recreation. They then expanded their lecture notes into volumes of their own and three times a year they poured out their acquired knowledge in three hour written examinations plus oral or vocal tests. If an exam was not passed then it had to be re-taken and failure to pass eventually meant another body trudging off to catch a bus.

This, however, was more flexible than the smoking rule. The professors soon got to know their students and their capabilities. A clever but lazy student could well be required to retake an examination even if, on sheer marks, he passed but did not excel. Another man could be judged to have worked hard and done his best but not to be sufficiently academic to shine or even to gain a pass mark. Repeated and abject academic failures would be given help and could, eventually, be advised to leave since it was accepted that future priests had to have something to keep their ears apart but did not have to be intellectually brilliant. St. John Vianney was an accepted warning to the authorities that an academic lame duck could turn out to be a good priest; and he was a great source of comfort and consolation to most of us in the first year or so when Philosophy remained more or less a closed book; partly because of the manner in which it was being taught.

Three morning lectures with a short break were the order of the day followed by lunch, a short prayer session and the half hour of recreation during which smoking was allowed and solitary swanning off was not tolerated. We were supposed to converse, get to know each other or try to keep up with the world by reading the one copy of the Daily Telegraph pinned up in the common room or listening to an old and solitary steam radio in the lower common room which was known as the 'den'. It was lower not because it catered for the less advanced members of the student body but because it was down in the cellar. It was called the 'den' because most smokers made their way into it to listen to the news, play at the one bald billiard table and generally behave less sedately than did the intellectuals up above.

Afternoons were not recreation time but periods for physical exercise in one form or another according to the old principle that a healthy body houses a healthy mind! - *'mens sana in corpore sano'* as old Juvenal said a long time ago. Football, tennis in season, hand-ball, a vicious game played against a wall with a hard ball which, as the name implies, was clouted with the hand (bare or gloved) and is probably responsible for the fact that my right hand is larger than my left, hockey and an esoteric game with bat and soft ball, unique to that seminary and which I never even tried to play or understand - all these could take up one or two afternoons during the week. One day could be spent on a profitable hobby such as gardening, leatherwork, book-binding or woodwork. Otherwise it meant either going for a run or for a walk; more of which later.

With luck a game of football or tennis or handball covered two or three of the afternoons each week. At least one afternoon could be spent legally doing some woodwork, two if one's memory was bad and conscience elastic. Gardening was out of the question in no time since, having acquired a strip round the back of the house (no mean feat this for a first year man since there was a waiting list) it soon became apparent that I knew nothing about it, had no idea what to plant and, having planted flowers or vegetables, they dramatically withered and died. One or two afternoons had to be killed by either running or going for a walk.

Both of these activities involved leaving the boundaries of the seminary and so had to be performed in groups of three or, at most, four. Each group led by at least one cleric, i.e. a man who not only had done two years in the place but was also at least on the lowest rung of the clergy - he had been tonsured. One signed out in a book which was carefully scrutinised so that the groups would not consist of the same individuals more often than now and again. Keeping the same company anywhere near too often was construed as 'particular friendships' and sternly frowned upon as not only essentially dangerous but also not conducive to training one to be able to mix with all and sundry. A run, therefore, had to be carefully planned. You had to arrange with at least two others who were doing it for the same reason - to have as short a run as possible, work up a sweat, get back and have a shower and then spend the rest of the afternoon period on the bed reading a murder book. If your group leader was a fitness fanatic then you had to do a five or six mile run and were ruined for days. If he was a good runner then you had to keep up or spoil the delight of the others by unduly slowing them down. If you chose with care and, eventually, experience, then you had three or four chaps jogging off at high speed, slowing down for a breather when out of sight and returning at a brisk trot to perform their ablutions and go to bed with an Agatha Christie.

The ultimate horror was to go for a walk. Again in group formation and depending on the taste or length of legs of the leader but added to this the rule that one had to wear black and wear a hat! Thus the natives, used to seeing these small groups emerge at regular intervals and set off in straight lines into the surrounding heath and countryside, called us ' *The Black Beetles'*. The only redeeming feature was the beauty of the countryside surrounding Wonersh; the open heath and parkland which, on a fine day, made the whole exercise just about bearable. Visits to a village shop were not allowed and to stop for a drink was unthinkable. Even to think of stopping for a half pint would bring instant dismissal. The rule was that only after having walked four miles as the crow flies could one stop for non-alcoholic refreshments. This, of course, also meant having to walk the four miles back.

The result of this rule was that every student knew, to a few yards, the bee line distance to any café or shop within that magic radius of four miles. The keen walkers actually achieved the distance on a good afternoon. The less keen did not attempt it. Some quickly acquired such a dislike of walking that they made a vow (which I still keep) of never walking anywhere if at all humanly possible once the far distant date of one's ordination came about. As to the hat, an expensive item, I bought mine at a seminary auction in aid of the Missions, it was the wrong size and would just perch precariously when exiting or re-entering the compound. I always carried it and it served to swat flies and other vermin encountered on such walks.

In the house and gardens all students wore a full cassock and collar and always wore a biretta. This, not to be confused with a Beretta as used by Agent 007 and licensed to kill, was - and still is - a square piece of hard headwear not designed for a round head. When walking, it had to be worn at all times. To be lifted when sighting a Professor or when passing a shrine or statue in corridors or garden. Another vow made was never to wear it again after ordination unless under pain of sin or in the sight of the Bishop during a solemn liturgy. Mine is now safely stowed in my coffin, still hard and square and utterly unfit for a head, to be confined with me to my grave.

Reflection

God has created me to do Him some definite service; He has committed some work to me which He has not committed to another. I have a mission – I never may know it ibn this life, but I shall be told it in the next. Somehow I am necessary for His purpose, as necessary in my place as an Archangel in his – if, indeed, I fail, He can raise another, as he could make the stones children of Abraham. Yet I hav a part in this great work; I am a link in a chain, a bond of connection between persons. He has not created me for naught. I shall do good, I shall do His work; I shall be an angel of peace, a preacher of truth in my own place, while not attending it, if I do but keep His commandments and serve Him in my calling

  Blessed John Henry Newman

In general, the rule and way of life verged on that of a prison. There were no bars, no physical restraints. What made it different from any prison was that these rules were accepted by young and old on a voluntary basis; they were worth the bother and tedium because of the desired purpose of one's existence in a seminary - to be a seedling, to be trained and grow and mature so as to be ordained after six years. Incidentally also, to learn something.

The mind boggles as to what effect such a regime had on young men still in the formation stage and allowing it to be imposed for six years. Perhaps it did very little harm, in fact. The times were different, one's expectations were different. People in general accepted things which now seem deplorable. It certainly did train one to accept restrictions if the end, the purpose, seemed worth-while. It also separated those who seemed to accept the rules as ends in themselves and those who saw them as a necessary nuisance and, in all kinds of little ways, tried and managed to get around them and keep to the letter if not always the spirit.

It was only years later that the unavoidable result became very clear: those, certainly in our year, who were fanatics at keeping the smallest rules - they wore their hat, they walked energetically, run frantically, gardened with utter zeal and never spent more than the allotted 20 minutes in their bath - were the first to give up their priesthood. Those who carefully picked their groups of like-minded lazy runners, carried their hats, dodged the column when they could, found inside woodwork jobs which meant they could keep warm seemed, on average, to survive the real life outside after ordination.

By 3.30 p.m. all would have returned from their exercise, work, sports or dodgy activities and, washed and cassocked, were ready for the afternoon lecture. At the end of this there was a frugal tea followed by total silence for private study. This was done in your room or in the library, alone, without the aid of discussions, seminars or other such distractions. For some two and a half hours one researched the background to notes taken at lecture, wrote up one's notes (wonder of wonders, typewriters were allowed!) synthesized one's new-found knowledge and set it up in such a way that when the end of term examination came one could regurgitate the fourteen ways of not understanding the mystery of the Trinity in a nearly robotic fashion. Again, nobody checked that you were working; there were no distractions of transistor radio, tape player, and gramophone or - God forbid - a portable T.V. One could have slept for the two hours but not only did pride forbid but the results in work not done would have been cumulative and, eventually, catastrophic. What better training, in many ways, could one have for the life of a priest in a parish when, in the long run, nobody actually checks or does any kind of time and motion study of one's work.

The day was regulated by the bell and 7.30 p.m. was thus announced to be followed by supper, which led to a half hour of compulsory recreation in common when one could have one's third and last smoke of the day, or - again - read the one copy of the 'Daily Telegraph' displayed in an old-fashioned stand in the upper common room or listen to the radio in the lower den. Until 9.30 p.m. time was our own - in a restricted sort of way. We could walk outside if it was not dark; stay in one's room or 'visit' other students. The word 'visit' is judiciously put in inverted commas since it did not mean actually entering someone's room. This space was sacrosanct. You could stand at the door and chat, one to one. No crowds of two or more at a door to gossip, discuss or even pray; and voices had to be hushed so as not to disturb others. At 9.30 the bell summoned one to Evening Prayers in chapel. By 10.00 p.m. all lights were out and all slept the sleep of the just, the exhausted, the weary, desperate, those punch-drunk by Philosophy, worried sick by fear of exams, 'blockings' or just happy to sleep.

And it is important to stress that this sort of regime did not lead to misery. It was, in many ways, a happy period of structured life, no worries about the day to day living expenses, busy with quite complicated studies, mutual support from one's fellow inmates and, above all, a period which was but a means to an end. It was a very different life in the world and the Church when things were accepted in a very different way. Each individual had made the decision to aim for ordination and was willing to accept all sorts of hardships and even stupid rules in order to achieve this. There were certainly periods of misery, times of doubt or rebellion, boredom and frustration. Anyone, however, who found the regime intolerable for any length of time would certainly either leave or become so obstreperous that he would be advised to leave. One became institutionalised to some extent, even to the degree that when the holidays came it was hard to re-adjust for the first day or so to a 'normal' way of life.

Looking back and with one's present knowledge and attitude there are many things which could have been done far better; especially the manner of teaching and learning. On the other hand, the training this sort of regime gave did make one 'bloody-minded' in the sense that if a thing had to be done, then it was done. It was a good preparation for what was to come when going into a parish as a curate; since curates at that time were still the lowest form of life in the Church. The regime may well have left traumas of all sorts; the manner of learning left a lot to be desired; six years spent in very full time education was never acknowledged by any sort of degree and left huge gaps in one's body of knowledge unless they were filled from a man's own reading and interests. The link with the outside world was a tenuous one through those years so that the Suez crisis had hardly any impact on us and I have no idea who won a cup final between 1953 and 1959. On the whole, however, and with some notable exceptions, it was a stretch of six years which did its job of formation and education and certainly cannot be forgotten nor its effects in the rest of one's life ignored or minimised.

This daily schedule - with slight variations for Sundays and Holydays - went on day after day with just two weeks off after Christmas and eight weeks off in the summer. Since it was the seminary of St. John and his feast day falls on December 27th, we had stay to celebrate that day with due solemnity, which meant, of course, that we could not be at home for Christmas. Since, however, out in the parishes few priests would be able to get 'home' or away on Christmas for the rest of their priestly lives this also was good training for the future. Christmas Day was celebrated with Midnight Mass and a very High Mass on Christmas Day itself and comparative freedom to do anything one liked - as long as it was on the premises - for the rest of the day. Traditionally, there was a whist drive and gramophone concert plus a Gilbert and Sullivan performed by the students. After the solemn Mass on St. John's Day and the lunch usually attended by the Bishop and higher flights of ancient clergy, we were all free to go.

Holidays at home were, again, expected to be spent either soberly by perhaps helping in the parish or, with special permission if the need was there, by working at some odd job - in keeping with one's lofty vocation - to earn enough cash to survive the rest of the year. Grants from educational authorities were unheard of for the priesthood at that time. Many of us simply had to find some work to get enough pocket money to get through the term. Food, lodging, laundry were provided. Books could be borrowed from the library. But transport back to the place had to be paid for and there were the small things such as stamps, toothpaste, boot polish, haircuts, soap, football boots - not to mention liniment for injuries sustained by the spectacularly rough and brutal fouls common among seminary teams - razor blades and innumerable other necessities all had to be paid for. Plus tobacco! An ounce of Three Nuns judiciously packed into a small pipe and smoked under strict control would last me nearly two weeks. Charlie - an ex-barber - did fine haircuts for 6 old pence (2 ½ new p) for the foreign missions and trained others to do the same. A razor blade, vigorously rubbed each day on a special curved glass block obtainable once for a lifetime of use in the seminary shop would last for a whole term. Alcohol never had the chance to pass our lips since there was no question of going out for a pint. Somehow, everyone survived and those who did happen to have wealth from home, good holiday jobs, savings from previous careers or obtained hard cash from rich relatives or supporters were certainly discouraged from flaunting it.

My own great and continued miracle was that throughout these years my Post Office savings account never dropped below Â£5! It was boosted by holiday earnings and then gradually declined as the weeks went by. Just before a crisis I always seemed to get a cash injection from my Parish Priest, Canon McHugh (who always promised or threatened to come and see me but never did until my ordination) or some utterly unexpected source. Such as getting pyjamas or socks from the Catholic Needlework Guild - which were invariably made for gorillas and thus were sold for hard cash to larger clerics. I even 'earned' the princely sum of five shillings (25 new pence) by having one of my feet washed on Maundy Thursday by the Rector - the traditional Maundy Money. This paid for 2 ounces of pipe tobacco - smoking for three weeks or so!

The spring and summer terms formed one long period of six months with no release except for Easter Monday which was the only day (apart from a student lying on his deathbed) when the family could come and visit. They could arrive after breakfast and stay until about 4.00 p.m. and take one out - individually and in a car! - between those times. In many ways, this day was to be dreaded rather than welcomed. It broke up a sustained period of institutional habit and it took a week to get settled in again. The good thing was that the family could see where their dearly beloved spent six years even though all kinds of quaint places and customs had to be explained to them.

The summer holidays lasted for eight weeks and some went off on continental and exotic jaunts. Others got all pious and helped out in shrines or places of pilgrimage, a few just sat around at home and did nothing while a goodly number found a job to fill their coffers for the next year. Each student had to report to their parish priest at home and bring back a report of their behaviour on holiday. Lack of such a report - or one stating that the lad had not been seen or been living any kind of ungodly life during this time - would certainly raise questions and, possibly, result in the equivalent of a red card and the early bath. Again, this made sense and was perfectly acceptable if one had nothing to hide.

The real problems arose with holiday work. Permission from the Rector had to be obtained and this was seldom given after the first two years when, normally, the clerical collar became compulsory at all times except in bed and the bath. This was after the reception of the 'Tonsure' - more of which hereafter. Fortunately for those of us from an outside Diocese this permission had to be obtained from our own Bishop. Leo Parker, by the grace of God and favour of the Apostolic See Bishop of Northampton, was a sensible and frugal man. He was not mean (he paid for my first cassock and continued my weekly pocket money allowance of 2/6 – (12 and a ½ new pence - throughout my first four years of training) but was more than willing to allow a student to work during the holidays and not have to wear the clerical collar while doing so. Thus in the Christmas holidays I did odd jobs for a grocery shop and/or filled in at the local Post Office sorting mail. During the summer I spent six of the eight weeks working from 7.30 in the morning to 5.00 at night cheerfully mixing soups in the Nestle factory at 1/6 an hour plus the perks of being able to buy coffee, chocolate and, of course, soups at rock bottom prices at the end of every week.

It was common enough for students in general to work in the holidays but the regular labour force would express great surprise when told what I was being trained for and horrified at the length of the training. Mixing soup was monotonous and soul-destroying for the first week or so. After that it became quite tolerable and was enlivened by the change of soups one had to mix - tomato, peas, oxtail, mushroom, onion or even celery. This last was the worst simply because the smell of celery remained on one's clothes and in one's pores more or less permanently. On getting home I used to leave my working togs in the garden shed, streak upstairs to have a bath and still smell and taste celery for the rest of the evening.

One old boy in the factory had been doing this same job for 25 years and was quite happy and contented but slightly deaf and forgetful. Whenever he asked what I was training for and was told it was 'for the priesthood' he always understood it was 'to be a policeman' and commented on how I was going to be a little one if I ever made it!

The second summer holiday - the first two weeks of it, anyway - was made unforgettable for me because, as the junior sacristan, I had the option of going back to help with the clergy retreats. My fare was paid plus the princely sum of £10 per week to prepare and help 50 or so priests of all ages while they made their annual retreat from Monday to Friday. Seeing them, all shapes and sizes, young and old, grotty and elegant, mumbling their Mass or saying it with devotion, eating - some of them quite disgustingly - very nearly put one off any idea of becoming a priest. The three or four volunteers who had decided to earn some money in this way were all and utterly appalled by the thought that, in years to come, they themselves might become like some of these priests. It was a very educational and salutary fortnight.

For two summer holidays I graduated from the more or less menial work of soup mixing to a white-collar job at the local office of H.M. Inspector of Taxes. Knowing my aspirations to the clerical state the local supervisor put me in charge of the section dealing with Church of England clergy tax returns. It could have been a golden opportunity to start yet a few more religious conflicts by mismanaging these returns but as far as I am aware there were no complaints and - for once - I must have done something right. The pay was marginally better than that earned by my soup making skills and the hours were shorter.

Back in the seminary the first two years were spent in studying Philosophy in all its branches with Scripture and Church History thrown in by means of two lectures each per week. Philosophers went out into the world - in aforesaid groups - wearing black ties, not clerical collars, and tended to look like undertakers. Since my hope was that the tie would only have to be with me for two years I never untied the knot so as not to wear the thing out. The result, at the end of that period, was the tiniest knot known to man; hard and solid and shiny.

Philosophy remained a closed book to most of us in spite of passing three examinations a year by regurgitating wisdom which an intelligent parrot could have coped with. It only came into its own when we started theology and lots of terms, definitions, ways of thinking, discussing and arguing started to make sense. Church History and Scripture were very poor relations and were taught by listening to lectures of 45 minutes each, never being allowed to discuss or, God forbid, ask a question, and having sheets of notes given to us which - word for word - reproduced the lectures. The result was that, except for a few dedicated students with incredible consciences, we did not listen to the lectures but wrote letters home, did other work, caught up on previous notes or even worked ahead on the subject and dealt with it in more depth. It is amazing what one can do by just sitting in a bench among a hundred others and looking vaguely intelligent. Yawns, chatting, head down in one's arms or other signs of distraction were the give-away to be avoided. On one famous occasion, the day after a general election when the results were coming out on the radio, an entrepreneur rigged up a wire and earphone from the wireless down in the den and a constant string of notes went round the lecture hall giving up-to-date state of the parties. To this day I am convinced that the lecturer knew what was going on but doggedly ploughed on regardless. He also rejoiced in the nickname of 'The Mole' because he was a small, shrivelled and very shy but charming man who never looked up throughout his rapid reading of his lectures.

The drop-out rate in those first two years was about a quarter. Mostly because a man realised he had no 'vocation' or was so informed by the Rector; a vocation being clearly defined as, 'the acceptance of a candidate by his Bishop' and in no way any inner or mysterious calling or urge or conviction that one ought to become a priest. Since Bishops and Rectors and other 'lawful superiors' could only judge by externals, this calling depended on one's behaviour at all levels and the general impression one gave to others. An Oscar-winning actor may have been able to keep up a front and play a part consistently enough to bring about such a conviction in others; perhaps some did. But it would have been incredibly difficult and rather pointless to one's future. Some were requested to leave for one or a string of misdemeanours or ordered to do so for something spectacularly evil (breaking bounds by going off on one's own into the village was about the only such crime known at the time. Nobody ever went off with one of the maids since they were specifically designed by age and shape and temperament not to present any temptation). A few left because they simply did not have the intellect even to pretend to understand Philosophy and found the study utterly impossible, and these were the ones who probably would have made the best priests and whose departure was usually regretted most.

One particular example of this was the departure of an elderly and lovable 'lay brother' from a religious novitiate about a mile from us. The custom was that the superiors decided who should get ordained - never mind the wishes of the individual - and they came to us for their intellectual preparation. This chap had been a happy lay brother for over 30 years and had no wish whatever to become a priest. He dutifully attended all the Philosophy lectures but when it came to the three hour written examination - and I was sitting next to him and scribbling away pouring out all my new-found knowledge - he simply put down his name and the date and then sat back and slept. When, at the end of the next term, he did exactly the same his superiors took the hint, had the wisdom to acknowledge their mistake and he cheerfully went back to his chosen way of life.

A very few were judged to be intellectually more than able but so obviously idle that they did no work whatever. One man left because even the mention of blood, childbirth or any part of the anatomy inevitably resulted in him fainting rather spectacularly. Some left solely because they were materially very well off and could not put up with the simplicity of life and the plethora of - very often pointless - rules.

Those who survived were then due to receive the first of the Minor Orders, or, more accurately, the Tonsure which officially made them into clerics. All these grades of orders are now part of history but at that time there was a solemn and much valued ceremony at the beginning of one's third year when the Bishop would brutally but liturgically cut off five bits of hair (representing the sign of the cross) and thus 'tonsure' a man as a sign that he was being given to God. Great hilarity was caused by those badly bald who had little to offer in this symbolic way and the Bishop needed a sharp eye to find five bits of hair on the man's scalp. At the other extreme, if a man had a fine head of curly hair, a fringe or quiff, then the Bishop took some delight in ruining his hairstyle for some months to come by hacking off - with very blunt, ceremonial, silver scissors - the new cleric's hirsute pride and joy.

The serious part of the ceremony was that it made one a cleric, part of the Church's hierarchy (though a very lowly one) and you were 'incardinated' i.e. started to belong to a Diocese. It also meant that the clerical collar had to be worn with the suit, one's tie could be handed on to some more junior student who was so desperate as to want a worn-out tie and one could become the leader of a group of walkers or runners for the afternoon constitutional. This, in practice, was the most important since it meant that you could choose two other members of reasonable attitude and decide how far to walk, where to go to, how fast to run and how soon to get back to savour the rest of the afternoon period. You also started to be called 'Reverend' in official lists and documents even though, face to face, the professors still called you 'Mister'. Never, throughout the six years, did a professor call a student by his Christian name.

Being 'blocked' was the dreaded event before tonsure and other minor or even major orders. This entailed putting off the acceptance into the reverend state of the clergy because of some doubt in the minds of the authorities as to one's ability and/or worthiness. It was not all that common but did happen every year and especially to those who belonged to the Southwark Diocese since the decision was made by the seminary authorities and rubber-stamped by the Bishop. We outsiders tended to be far less worried about this because if the Bishop of Northampton or Nottingham or whatever was to be told that his student had what we now call 'an attitude problem' he would either scoff or decide to sack the man himself. Blocking was a method of getting a student to pull his socks up but more often than not resulted in a man leaving and giving up. If someone were to be really considered to be unsuitable then they would be asked to leave and this odd method of encouragement would not be employed.

It is now only of historical interest but at that time, after the Tonsure, candidates for the Priesthood had to go through a series of minor orders - Lector and Porter, Exorcist and Acolyte, followed by the Sub-diaconate and then the Diaconate, which led to ordination. These were conferred through the next four years in interesting ceremonies when the newly acquired 'office' had to be ceremonially exercised; the Lector did some reading, the Porter opened and locked the church door and rung the bell, the Acolyte (officially the only one who had the duty and 'power of orders' to serve Mass) carried a candle. But, fortunately, the Exorcist did not have to cast out any devils; he was simply given the power and authority to do so, but only with the expressed permission of his Bishop.

The sub-Diaconate was a strange sort of order since it did not confer anything in particular. It was more a braces and belt effort to delay the positive step of becoming a Deacon; just in case the candidate changed his mind or his Bishop changed his. The only obvious duty a sub-deacon had was to participate in Solemn High Masses in full and special vestments (but without a stole) and spend a goodly amount of time standing still, wearing a humeral veil and holding the paten. (If you are not familiar with these technical terms - look up a good dictionary). A Deacon, on the other hand, took the formal step of being permanent, accepting the law of celibacy and being given the power to preach, teach, officiate at baptisms and - above all - distribute Holy Communion. He was invested with a stole - officially the priestly vestment - but worn on one shoulder only. (The symbolism seems to be that a deacon assumes only part of the burdens of a priest who, assuming them all, wears the stole on both shoulders). At that time there were no Eucharistic Ministers and it was considered grossly improper for anyone other than priest or deacon to touch a consecrated Host under any but utterly extreme circumstances (one of which was always quoted as being acceptable: if a Host was accidentally dropped down the cleavage of a lady communicant then neither priest nor deacon should not - ever - grope for It!)

The first year was, perhaps naturally, the most difficult. Most of those who left did so during that time although some gave the whole thing only a matter of weeks and left in the first term while others got cold feet three or four years into the course or even - on some rare occasions - just before the Diaconate. Time went by quite quickly in an ordered life to which one adapted. It was not all work, prayer and misery. There were plenty of opportunities for hobbies, reading, music, plays and Gilbert and Sullivan [there is an infamous picture still around of the cast of 'Iolanthe' with myself in the title role as a fairy. Make-up thickly applied worked wonders but it took a long time to live down the disgrace that, at the dress rehearsal, my first entrance was made with me - supposedly a fairy - still wearing glasses!] as well as sport and, above all, time for, with and by oneself. The rule which barred others from one's room was a great blessing since otherwise a lot of privacy would have been lost to the more garrulous types and time would have been wasted making coffee, playing pontoon or even [the one thing that could have been useful and not a waste of time] just discussing the subjects being taught. There was no television except on rare state occasions when one was hired for the whole community. We did not have transistor radios, record players, kettles, toasters or access to telephones.

A new priest with my mother and my sister

Chapter III

Ordination at Corby

The year and day of ordination was marked off from the start and acted as a sort of beacon towards which one aimed and its approach seemed to accelerate as the years went by. Some had a most romantic notion of the whole thing and really harboured the ambition to save the world once ordained. Some did look on it as a career, in a good sense, and spoke openly of having a large parish or even reaching the higher flights of the hierarchy. Some, the intellectuals, looked forward to further studies in Rome or Paris and quite openly saw themselves as returning to the seminary as professors. Most of us - and all tended to gather into like-minded groups in spite of all the phobia about 'particular friendships' - simply battled on to learn what we could, pass exams, keep our noses clean and looked on the day of ordination as a reward for six years effort.

What all did share was a practically total ignorance of what life would really be like 'out in the parish'. We all knew the theory of starting off as curates, we knew the sort of work to be done in parishes, we listened to horror stories of the cruelty of parish priests but did not really believe them. The expectations of priestly work were clear and seemed to be unchanging. We knew what would be expected of us in general terms, the jobs of curates, parish priests, chaplains; the whole idea of celibacy which was simply accepted as a necessary condition for ordination; the concept of obedience as accepting the job given by the Bishop etc. There was very little rumbling of discontent on important issues and no inkling in 1959 of the tremendous changes which would be unleashed on the Church by the Vatican Council and that the world outside was changing more and more rapidly in general.

Money - or the lack of it - was a constant problem to most of the students even though all the necessities were paid for by the Diocese and there was little or no opportunity to spend on entertainment, drink or outings. The holiday wages I earned went mainly on transport. I had to make sure that there was enough money in the kitty to get home for the summer. Spending was restricted to the strictly controlled and - now accepted as evil - habit of smoking and the odds and ends which one needed for stamps to keep contact with the outside world, soap etc to keep handsome and hygienic and the purchase of paper, ink, typing ribbon (amazing how often the old fashioned sort could be run and re-run through a portable typewriter) and frugal sweets such as Polo mints. The odd thing was that whenever I reached rock bottom in finances - which meant that only £5 were left in the Post Office book - either the old Canon from Aylesbury or some other kind and usually unexpected benefactor would send a postal order or note and things would look up again. Or the Catholic Needlework Guild sent some pairs of socks, pyjamas or shirt to worthy students. These were invariably made for gorillas so that I resold them to bigger students and solved my financial problems for another few weeks. Mr. Micawber was my patron saint and I never went below the Â£5 in the savings book [which also brought in 2 Â½% interest per annum - 6 old pennies per Â£1]. My last two years were spent in comparative opulence: Bishop Parker had negotiated a grant from some obscure Irish society rejoicing in the name of St. Joseph's Young Priests' Society and based in Dublin. Every quarter thenceforth I received a postal order for Â£10 and the first letter I wrote after ordination was to thank the Society and assure them that I had made it - just.

Just - because throughout the six years - as before and ever since - I have never had the luxury of God whispering in my ear that he wanted me to be his priest. It seemed a good idea at the time and every beginning and end of term it seemed not such a good idea and I used to tell my long-suffering spiritual director that I reckoned I ought to give up. He invariably agreed that I would not be the answer to any heartfelt prayer by Holy Mother Church but advised that I should pray a bit and wait for a week or two before making the final decision. In the blind confidence that a vocation came from the call of one's superiors rather than a St.Paul-like divine voice near Damascus we repeatedly agreed that I ought to carry on.

The hurdle of Philosophy and the Tonsure having been cleared the next four years were occupied with the study, first, of Fundamental Theology (a sort of introduction to and reasoned defence of theology) together with Dogmatic Theology, Moral Theology and Canon Law. Plus, of course, still the Church History and Scripture both with their continued drawbacks of their manner of being taught. Again, the system was the same: sit and listen, take notes, research, write up notes, learn for the examinations but never discuss, ask questions or - God forbid - be asked to write an essay or air one's views. The nit-picking in trying to solve insoluble mysteries of the Trinity or Real Presence took up so much time that complete other tracts of theology were never really covered. Equally, the morality of thoughts, deeds, omissions, intentions and wildly inventive case histories never really made moral theology something positive or practical. The tract on sex (!) had to be studied from a text book written in Latin since the vernacular would have made the book more obscene for that period than 'Lady C's Lover' and, no doubt, would have produced a court case sooner or later. Case histories were always lurid, mythical and the female in the case was always called 'Bertha'.

Canon Law was, at least, a cut and dried science where every word and phrase had a meaning and any reasonable interpretation could be justified and argued by reference to the principles of law. In many ways each discipline impinged on the others and, at last, the Philosophy we had suffered in the first two years came into its own by giving us the understanding of technical terms and a discipline of thought and argument which made the rest possible; even if not exactly easy. The volume of study and knowledge and literature through the centuries on all these subjects is incredible and in all languages under the sun, from Greek and Hebrew through Latin to the notoriously learned, heavy and stodgy Germans who must be the most thorough of all scholars and make for the most tedious reading.

In an establishment of over a hundred students plus some fifteen professors there are innumerable jobs that have to be done to keep the place running smoothly, cooking, washing up, laundry and cleaning of the house in general was under the supervision of nuns with the help of maids and general help from the local

Community. The cleaning and general order of one's room depended on the individual and, again, was presumed to be done properly without having to be supervised. All other jobs to do with study, the liturgy, the welfare of students, entertainment, general maintenance, sport, were farmed out to students on a very rigid basis of seniority and growing responsibility. Few, if any, went through the six years without some 'public' duty even if only for a year or so.

The claim was that, after the first year of getting to know the students, such jobs would be dished out according to the abilities, gifts or needs of individuals. Whether by luck or judgement the job I was landed with was sacristan - a four year stint which progressed from the first year doing menial jobs such as cleaning brass and lighting candles to the lofty status of head sacristan who was in overall charge, opened and locked church and safe, ordered everything for the liturgy and was generally regarded as one of the elite.

This four year job probably did me more good in the long run than all the rest of the training and learning in the whole of the six years. From being excruciatingly shy and dreading standing out in any way in a crowd or even the company of two or three others, I became capable of appearing and acting in public. Not in any way with ease or without a care or thought, but as a result of realising that shyness is a very obvious form of pride and arrogance and can be overcome by determination and by careful preparation so that whatever one is going to do in public is all organised beforehand.

Cleaning brasses was no problem; just a bore. But going out in front of everyone to light candles the first few times was a heroic deed, especially if a candle would not light or the taper went out. The lesson learnt was that candles had to be so prepared that they would light; a taper had to be carried so that it would not blow out; Obvious, perhaps, but a most valuable lesson.

One then progressed to looking after other parts of the church, the vestments, the laundry, the altar cloths which had to be perfect and eventually take full responsibility for everything including the mistakes or slackness of more junior sacristans. In comparison to many jobs done in the outside world by a young man of 22 or 23 these responsibilities were slight; but in their context and under the eyes of a crowd of critical students and watchful staff, fastidious and often fanatical liturgical experts, the job had to be done right and was a marvellous training for getting rid of shyness plus gaining a determination to do things properly. It also, incidentally, had some perks; such as not having to join the seasonal potato picking and having one afternoon a week free from the above mentioned physical exercises so as to do this particular job. As head sacristan you also had a lot more flexibility in what one could do and when; one had the keys of the whole place and a reasonable extension as to getting to bed at night and a more friendly relationship with the authorities based on mutual need and trust.

The job did teach a lot about the liturgy which in those days was far more complex and defined than it is now. [There was, and perhaps still is, a liturgical bible generally known as *Fortescue O'Connell* which laid down every action and every detail of every liturgical ceremony. It also boasted the infamous footnote stating: *'Bishop now enters wearing skullcap only'*]. By luck or common sense I never got too involved in the gory details and sometimes quite heated arguments about liturgical fashions. But the job of sacristan also brought about at least one quite hilarious situation when, on locking up at night, one had to go through the length of the whole, quite long, chapel in total darkness to get back into the house through the internal rear door. This was achieved by walking straight down the centre aisle towards the reflection of the sanctuary lamp in the picture of the Pope hanging right at the back of the church. Two steps to the left on reaching this plus one forward and the door was there. This worked quite infallibly except for the night when there was a coffin in the middle of the aisle containing the stout body of a deceased Monsignor who was destined to be buried in the small graveyard next morning. He made it; but only just. Forgetting that the coffin was there and walking boldly straight down the middle I encountered the coffin with my midriff, was badly winded and knocked the Very Reverend off his catafalque. The coffin, fortunately, did not split. Recovering from the shock and putting on some lights I heaved him with some difficulty and great danger of a hernia back into place and no lasting harm was done.

Another boost to morale and/or remedy for shyness or conviction that one could not do things in public was being made a 'pluvialist' to the Rector for all the most solemn occasions. This meant that you had to have some sort of voice for the odd intoning at Mass or solemn Vespers and that you wore a full cope, had to know when and how to bow, use the thurible and generally support and help the celebrant in a worthy and dignified manner - all, again, under the scrutiny of a hundred pair of eyes of all the students in the place and the critical approval, or not, of those who knew the liturgical bible backwards and regarded the rules as sacred.

The Rector was a little man of some girth but with tremendous dignity and awareness of his position (he eventually became the Bishop of Brentwood). He thus chose two little fellows to be his assistants and expected the same dignified bearing from them. Charlie was the other one. Ten years older than myself, an ex-barber who had left school at 14 and, on eventually deciding to become a priest, had sold his business and used the money to learn Latin and catch up on what are now called 'humanities' with a two year stay at a monastery, he found the intellectual part of the six years a real burden. He and I lived in next door rooms for six years, shared the bottom of the house list with the other Charlie (the Gibraltar one), had similar attitudes to walks and physical exercises and found the whole of the 'pluvialist' (a word which I have never managed to get the exact meaning of) business a great strain on our sense of dignity. Charlie was short, but also very thin, with hardly any shoulders to bear the cope with confidence. A special set of vestments proudly inherited from a rich donor from Rome and consisting practically completely of very stiff cloth of gold eventually brought our career as Rector's assistants to an inglorious end. On solemnly entering the chapel and genuflecting poor Charlie disappeared from view and left the cope standing under its own rigidity with no head sticking out of the top. This performance brought the house down, caused irrepressible giggles to him and equal mirth to myself and earned us both an official rebuke on the Rector's study carpet and, shortly afterwards, the sack from that particular job.

Mirth and enjoyment was not lacking in what would nowadays seem an incredibly artificial regime. There were many simple things we enjoyed even without television, radio, newspapers or visits to the pub. On looking back, the time went by incredibly quickly; possibly because of the rigid structure which made all of us very aware of where we stood, what was expected of us and, above all, what we were aiming for. Eventually the time came to prepare for ordination; having received all the minor orders and the Diaconate, learned all the theory that was available and very little practice. It would have been unheard of to follow the modern system of sending a Deacon into a parish for a few months to see life and work in the real world.

We never practised baptising a baby or doing a wedding. Sermons were preached once or twice a term to a group of fellow students. The script had to be written out, vetted by a professor and then preached parrot-fashion or read out to the small audience who took notes and then criticised content, delivery and manner. Every sermon had about four or five weeks of careful preparation, polishing and perfecting.

Nobody said, and we innocents never even imagined or suspected, that out in a parish there would have to be at least a sermon a week - often more. We did, once each, baptise a doll. This, quite naturally, did not squirm or yell, it did not have manifold chins which had to be lifted for the anointing of the little chest nor did it have thick hair into which the water soaked and trickled into the eyes and there were no parents or family standing around listening to an all Latin service.

What we did do was to practise the saying of Mass under the eyes of a specially chosen friend or server who week after week, for six months, would check every word, every action and gesture so that it conformed with the rubrics.

Rubrics were - still are - the rules laid down for every public liturgical act; and especially the Mass. They are so called because they were printed in red and they used to be unequivocal: *'The priest does this, says that'*. Now they are flexible (*'the priest may do this or that or other'*) to such an extent that each priest's Mass can vary widely in gestures, length and peripheral words. The essentials, of course, stay the same.

There were three kinds of *'voices'* that had to be used: loud, audible and secret. Three different bows: profound, deep and of the head only. Signs of the cross on oneself and the spreading of hands for prayer had to be at a certain level and within the confines of one's width of shoulder. The signs of the cross above the chalice or altar could - wonderful to relate, we had a choice - be either horizontal or at an angle of 45% but had to be consistent. One's thumbs had to be firmly and properly joined to one's first finger on both hands from the moment of Consecration until after their purification after Communion. The words had to be as the missal intended - in Latin, of course, with the proper Ciceronian accent and not the English public school pronunciation or the fizzy sound of the

French clergy; who always sounded like leaking lemonade bottles.

Eventually a '*dry mass*' (simulated, since one had not yet been ordained) was said under the eagle eye of the appropriate professor and if he approved then one was ready for ordination. It was traditional that the server and supervisor of all this for a Deacon was a year below him and thus learning a lot himself and the beauty of the hierarchy system in the sacristy was not just that we were specially familiar with amices, cinctures, stoles, maniples, dalmatics and tunicles, chasubles and copes, chalices, patens, ciboria, pyxes, lunettes, cruets, purificators, palls and corporals - not to mention tabernacles, torches, acolyte candles, sanctuary lights and the ideal number of candles (made of at least 65% beeswax) to be displayed on special days and special occasions - but also 'served' the ex-sacristan about to be ordained and were, in turn, served by the sacristan who was next in line after oneself. No modern priest - since the vernacular has come in and the rubrics have become a matter of choice - can imagine just how rigid the rules were and how every priest celebrated Mass in exactly the same way, which, of course, allowed no personal projection or variety, but also brought about great dignity and never caught either priest or people off balance by something unexpected. By the end of the practices every sign and gesture was automatic and in no way had to be thought about so that it could not take away from devotion or attendance to the words and their meaning. There was, as so often in all of this, some sense and method to apparent madness.

Ordination was, of course, the ultimate aim and took place on the Saturday after the feast of Pentecost. It was a ceremony lasting some four hours, all in Latin, which could not be left for any reason (faints, calls of nature included) under pain of excommunication (!) and most were ordained in the seminary chapel. A few chose or were chosen to be ordained in their parish and those from outside the Diocese more often than not went off to their cathedral or parish to be 'done' by their own Bishop. I was given the choice of either being ordained in the chapel or joining the Franciscans and be ordained by my own Bishop Parker with them. I had nothing against Franciscans [they had done their best to educate me for six years at Buckingham] but would have been surrounded on the day by strangers. I chose, together with eight others, to be ordained at the seminary by the Bishop of Southwark.

Chapter IV

Ordination and Corby

Some candidates became nervous wrecks after spending weeks and months preparing as if for a wedding. Chalices were inspected and bought, even specially commissioned. Visitors were invited and plans made for the first Mass back in the parish followed by ordination breakfast and general and wide celebration and rejoicing. Sacristans seemed to be traditionally hard-boiled and inured to such distractions and I especially simply looked forward to the event as being the end of six years of seminary life. We were allowed 40 visitors each to occupy special places in tiers in various parts of the chapel. Some needed far more than that so my popularity rating soared for the event since I was only having two visitors and was willing to sell my allotted seats at one ounce of pipe tobacco each. I arranged to say one of the normal Sunday Masses in the church in Aylesbury with the old Canon to assist me and simply to go back home afterwards for a normal breakfast. The princely sum of £32 sterling was collected by the parish before the ordination and with this I bought a chalice and a pyx which I still have and use (some bought a chalice for over £500, hand-made and incorporating their mother's engagement ring or other precious jewel. From my years of cleaning chalices I knew that anything with a jewel or a carving presents constant problems; and avoided that trap).

The ceremony was not a test of nerves. I knew what I was doing and even noticed promising obedience to the wrong Bishop and his successors but judged it to be a mere blip and not worth making a fuss about. I did smash my pocket watch at the prostration for the litany of the Saints [which was a most uncomfortable and dangerous exercise. It is very hard to know one's length when having to lie face down from a standing start. This meant that, before the ceremony, you had to practise just where your head would be, on a cushion, from that standing start. A judicious line drawn on the carpet ensured that as you prostrated you not only hit the cushion but also avoided smashing into the boots of the bloke in front of you.] I got the length right but forgot that the watch was in my waistcoat pocket and some twelve stone of dead weight would land on it - with the predictable result. It has never been the same since. My first blessing to my mother and sister was performed impeccably and gratefully for the years they had sacrificed so much to make the day possible. The greatest shock - even though expected - was the professors (aloof and distant for six years) suddenly calling me 'Father' or, even more traumatically, not 'Mister' but by one's Christian name!

After a very late breakfast/lunch [still fasting from midnight before Holy Communion at that time] in the staff room all the newly ordained priests departed with their guests. Gratefully even though with some regrets at leaving friends and a world which had guarded and cocooned one for so long, a structured life which needed little thought and expected even less initiative. And with some dread - although, thankfully, not full awareness - of the future in a parish. Most would have a holiday of some weeks or even months and would then be appointed to a parish or even sent on for further studies. I knew not only where I was going - to Corby, 'Occupation Road', ominously - but also that because of the state of health of the parish priest there I would have to be in place a week after ordination and look forward to a holiday some-time in the indeterminate future. A nice touch was the letter from the Bishop hand-written to inform me of this and, on the day of ordination, a telegram of congratulations from the parish priest whom I had never met but to whom I had been appointed as junior curate.

The next week passed quickly enough with my first Mass in Aylesbury parish church on the Sunday and further Masses in convents and surrounding parishes where they had never seen a newly ordained priest '*since the Reformation*', as the local paper had it. The embarrassing bit was the custom of people kissing the hands of such a priest after his blessing. After a week or so this gradually stopped and the only thing was to remember to react when someone called you 'Father' since that was a title to which one was not accustomed to respond.

The anti-Modernist oath was a screed of some three pages of inscrutable Latin instituted by Pope Pius X in his successful fight against the heresy of Modernism at the beginning of the 19 hundreds. We had to take this oath before being ordained a Deacon and then, again, before we received our faculties as a priest. For the ordination of a priest is simply a sacrament which confers the power to say Mass and to bless and absolve; it specifically stated in the ceremony that we could not exercise this truly momentous gift, gained but never earned through the past six years, without permission from our Bishop (except in the case of danger of death). This permission was what was known as the *'Faculty'* given by the Diocese. Somewhere I have a document stating that this has been given to me, renewed annually at the discretion of the Bishop and eventually - now - granted to all priests unless specifically withdrawn, which is more than can be said of a certificate of ordination. There is none. Apart from memory and some photographs, perhaps a list in the archives of the seminary and/or diocese, I cannot prove I have been ordained, just as I cannot prove - by recourse to my place of baptism, since it has been destroyed - that I have been baptised. In the unthinkable eventuality that I did not get baptised then my ordination is not even worth the photographs or memories!

The reception of the Faculty explains why Saturday, May 30th, 1959 about 4.00 p.m. and just a week after my ordination I was to be found solemnly kneeling in front of the fireplace in the Presbytery of Our Lady's, Occupation Road, Corby, reading through the oath and understanding it as little as I did on the original occasion a year or so before. Witnesses to this less than earth shattering event were the Parish Priest and his curate who both sat comfortably having a smoke while

I laboured through the Latin text and duly signed the oath, all this to enable me to go into the confessional box at 5.00 p.m. for the routine Saturday Confessions - 5.00 p.m. to 7.00.

To say that this was a traumatic experience is a massive under-statement. Obviously, there was no possibility of previous experience of hearing confessions. The theology of it all was that a priest is there not just to forgive but also to be a judge, a doctor and healer, a teacher and instructor and an adviser and consoler. A practical hint was to take the words of absolution - in Latin, of course - into the confessional in black and white since no matter how you might think you know them by heart, when it comes to the crunch you may well forget them. Armed with all this profound knowledge and a slip of paper I marched down the very long church of Our Lady to the confessional right at the back of the church; a sort of primitive horse-box reserved for the junior curate with five or six benches of penitents waiting and all looking at this young, slim and handsome cleric trying to exude confidence; not to say judicious sanctity of life and wisdom and experience. Children, men and women, young and old all itching to do their religious duty of weekly or fortnightly confession and get away for their Saturday night activities.

Corby in 1959 had just one Catholic Church and a new parish just starting in a developing district and still based on a school hall. Our Lady's claimed Easter duties of 2714 in 1960 and this would have been a pretty exact number since the Easter confessions were, in fact, counted one by one. Just to remind the young and innocent: this meant that between Ash Wednesday and Trinity Sunday - a matter of 14 weeks - that number of people went to confession at least once. Let's say 193 per Saturday. It was, of course, a lot more since many did go every week or two or three but were not then counted as 'Easter Duties' after the first time, of these souls some 90% were from Scotland with a firm Irish foundation and a genuine piety which, however, did not help with their peculiarly Corby/Scottish accent. It is absolutely true that quite apart from natural nerves and inexperience on my part things were made quite impossible by my inability to understand the whispered peccadilloes, sins or even crimes coming through the hole in the wall for the next two hours or so - non-stop. I confidently gave out penances according to the length of the list of sins rather than its content and absolved everyone without hesitation. My attempt to give a little and well prepared 'ferverino' was soon thwarted by a banging on the door by the parish priest telling me that I was taking too long per sinner and that the queue was increasing outside my box rather than decreasing. By 7.15 or so the door stopped opening and shutting and, after a pause, I carefully emerged from the box to find the church empty, myself utterly punch-drunk and late for supper.

When you think about it, two minutes for each confession means that the end of the second bench of patient penitents (say number 12 since one can reckon on six in a bench according to the usual architect's allowance of 18 inches per bottom) would be there and waiting for 20 minutes. Weekly confession was by no means a rarity at that period and with the opening and shutting of the door, kneeling down, sometimes in slow motion due to arthritis or devotional slowness, an introduction by the sinner, often with some hesitation whether the previous confession was one or two weeks away, a short list of sins and imperfections and a brief statement "for these and all my other sins which I cannot now remember I am sorry" there was not all that much time left to teach, inspire, heal or console plus giving a penance and a Latin absolution consisting of two prayers.

In time I did manage to understand things like 'wee wains greetin' as the vernacular for 'small children crying'. When some stated: 'I missed' it meant they had not been at Mass on the previous Sunday. By diligent questioning one probably found that they had been genuinely ill but still felt guilty and no matter how often they were assured of their innocence they still preferred absolution. Children (then aged 6 when making their First Holy Communion) quite often came in and said nothing. After some coaxing and encouragement a little voice well below the hole in the wall would go through the Ten Commandments - including adultery - and accuse itself of the lot. Some spoke up as if shouting orders in the steelworks blast furnaces while others whispered into my right, confessional and even then partly deaf ear so that all I got was a sibilant hiss as of a slightly irked snake.

The miracle of the sacrament at that time was not just that a priest could sit, solidly, for five hours (as I did at my first Christmas Eve confessional marathon) and not get ratty with the awkward squad but that the people had a simple faith in forgiveness and they did confess, repent and try to improve. It very soon became clear that there were many who lived incredibly holy lives with problems and hardships which were mind-boggling. In many cases the absolution was more a blessing or even a thanksgiving prayer rather than a sponge wiping away dirty spots and blotches on the soul. The simple faith in God and their trust in the wisdom of the priest of so many people was something which never ceased - or ceases - to amaze and often frighten me with the responsibility it imposes.

Reflection

Heavenly Father We put into our practical theology your grace and salvation, by stressing love of God and neighbour rather than the craven fear and awe of God and 'tooth for a tooth' attitude to that restricted concept of our neighbour as those of the same ilk as ourselves . We accept that God created a perfect universe, since it comes from a perfect being.

Father Stan [from his writings - The Ark]

The next day, Sunday, consisted of five morning Masses starting at 6.30 a.m. I was not required to preach that day but had to be present at all Masses to hear a sermon on the Priesthood and have the solemn blessing and kissing of hands. I did have to sing the 11.00 a.m. main Mass and be present at afternoon Benediction so that everyone would have the opportunity of seeing the Parish's new acquisition.

At lunch that day - an immutable 1.00 p.m. - I had my first brush with the parish priest because the housekeeper actually asked me what I would like for my dessert. This was due much more to my loving attitude to her little dog than any inherent charm on my part or her love of the clergy. This poor little pooch was hounded by the then Dean (later to become a Canon) who boasted that he once met him on the stairs and booted him down and straight through the front door. Being offered a choice of dessert went contrary to the accepted custom that the housekeeper was there for the parish priest alone and would only be allowed to tolerate such lowly creatures as curates.

Perhaps as a direct result of this clash I was told that I was to do the Baptisms at 3.00 p.m. This was a weekly event when whatever turned up, with or without notice, was small, preferably loud and accompanied by family (usually extended), got baptised in Latin and entered into the register. Having only once baptised a doll in the privacy of the seminary and an audience of two or three fellow students I was unprepared for a crowd of ten babies of assorted sexes, ages and vocal capacities accompanied by lots of children and adults who had to be sorted out according to who belonged to whom and who were parents, god-parents, just an audience or doting grandparents. The whole ceremony took very nearly two hours and the pious were already coming in for Benediction at 5.00 p.m. by the time I finished and left it to the mercy of God and efficacy of the sacramental system whether there were ten new Christians or not. Evening Mass had at that time not been invented so here was a shortish gap of inactivity until supper - dead on 7.00 p.m. That, I cheerfully presumed, was the end of the day and the rest of the night would be all mine! No way! By 10.00 p.m. it was expected that both curates be downstairs with their parish priest watching the television which, mercifully at that time, used to end shortly after 11.00 p.m. with a dot of light disappearing into itself and a voice saying: "Don't forget to switch off your set". It was then my duty, as junior curate, to do just that. To this day the tune advertising Fairy Liquid (*'The hands that do dishes can be soft as your face'*) brings back vivid memories of youth, the 'old man' and what, in time, became a quite pleasant evening ritual of mostly silent companionship.

To be fair, the old man (all of 59 or 60 at the time) insisted on this as a means of keeping in touch with his curates and making them feel at home. He sat there with a whisky, the senior curate had a gin and I eventually graduated to a Jumbo Stout imported free from the Catholic Men's Club next door for that very purpose. Unfortunately the conversational prowess of the parish priest was very limited and watching the box inhibited whatever temptation there may have been to discuss things. In time the silence became quite companionable and after a few years I could sit with him for an hour and we would both be quite content not to talk at all. He did, however, honestly think that this invariable nightly procedure was a fatherly and caring way of looking after his young men. When the box was switched off we all got up, locked up, trooped upstairs and wished each other a 'good night' and retired to bed.

Curates had one right - that of Christian burial. By law and custom they lived in the house 'owned' by the parish priest, run by his housekeeper who was employed by him and principally for him. The curate kept to the house rules set for him with no consultation and no discussion or court of appeal. By the age of 25 a highly educated young man was given a bed-sitter, a set of rules, rigid times and menus of meals and expectations of rising and going to bed at certain times while his friends whom he vaguely remembered from school were, by then, fathers of families, held down good jobs and enjoyed mortgages. The salary of a curate was £70 per year with board and lodging free. Any offerings for weddings and baptisms as well as the customary Christmas and Easter offerings were the property of the parish priest and only shared at his pleasure. A curate had to get the Bishop's permission to purchase a car and, as Bishop Leo maintained, this was not easily given since most curates wanted a car to get out of the parish rather than use it to work in the parish! As it happened, my parish priest was a very just man and shared the money equally and was not mean in any way. He had a genuine care for his curates but also a strict manner of imposing this with his own way and will and a manner which was bound to conflict with men a generation or more younger than himself. In short, he meant well but it took a long time and a lot of forbearance to recognise this.

Just as a curate only had the one right so he usually had only one ambition - to get his own parish; get his feet under his own table. The time span for achieving this could vary from an average of nine or ten years in our Diocese to twenty or twenty five years in Southwark or some of the northern Dioceses. It was even worse in Ireland (although often the curate had a house or flat of his own) where the story goes that a priest of 65 had just arrived back home after having retired from England to find that the priest in his parish was 66 and had just reached the lofty status of a parish priest. All these things were simply facts of life. Curates grumbled, they wished for better things, they lived for the future; but nothing could be done about it and, most probably, did not do as much harm as may now appear. Things had to run their course and change gradually - and not always for the better.

Everything, therefore, depended on the parish priest and life could be good, tolerable or downright impossible at the whim of one person. Curates themselves could be impossible and rebellious and so were moved off; usually at a week's notice. They received a letter from the Bishop simply telling them that from next week their services would be required elsewhere. It was not uncommon even in this Diocese (which had fewer priests than most and was growing and starting new parishes and thus the average years of a curacy tended to be eight or nine) for a curate to be in four or five parishes before having his own.

In a parish the size of Our Lady's, the new recruit was the junior curate, and thus even a lower form of life in an institution very much geared to a hierarchy. Looking back forty years plus it is clear that in many ways, according to the circumstances prevailing at that time, I was incredibly blessed and lucky! To begin with, the senior curate was a man in his early thirties, ordained some four years and incredibly kind and understanding as well as willing to give advice and help. He had been in the Army and was an unusual personality, much liked by the parishioners, given to bad language when irked but with a realism and sense of humour and willingness to buck the system. Unfortunately he went off on his annual holiday three weeks after my arrival and then disappeared off the face of the earth. Literally, nobody ever really found out what happened to him except that he had obviously planned not to return. All kinds of rumours did, naturally, spread but nothing conclusive nor more scandalous than that he had become a shepherd in Devon or Cornwall.

The result was that within four or five weeks of my elevation to the priesthood I became a senior curate! The old man, not all that well already, got really sick, blamed himself for not looking after his vanished curate properly and took to his bed determined to make sure that his new protégé would not go astray one inch. We received the help of a Dutch priest with a limited knowledge of English and I ran the parish. Not as an independent agent but a dogsbody governed from a sickbed by a very unhappy parish priest who not only told me what to do and how to do it but also took it for granted that I would do it wrong and listened to any reports of my activities with deep suspicion and fear that the place would fall apart and that he would be blamed - as he suspected, quite wrongly, that he was being blamed for the disappearing act of his senior curate.

The Dutch priest sent to us to help out was a good man, ordained some years already, but belonged to a religious order, not to the Diocese. He said the required Masses and visited the people and was very much liked by them. But he was not trusted with the important parts of the parish - money - and his limited English meant that I had to help him write his sermons and he was unable to instruct converts and heard confessions at a snail's pace. He also had nothing to lose or gain by keeping to arbitrary house rules; he did not rely for a good report to the Bishop and did not have to worry about gaining a reputation of being a 'difficult curate' - a tag which once gained could take at least two priestly generations to lose again. He thus did his work well, was helpful and sympathetic but was not expected to take any responsibilities and showed this by consistently appearing in the old man's room for the evening 'social happy hour' promptly at 10.00 p.m., having a gin (neat!) and then getting up and politely wishing us " Good night, Fathers" and going off for a good night's kip. He was not even attached to doorbell or telephone to answer sick calls at night. He stayed with us for some ten months, his English flourished; we got on very well and kept in touch for years remembering our odd existence with some affection. He eventually went to work in Singapore and is surely, by now, a retired gentleman like myself or, even, may have died.

My job, from the day of departure of the senior curate, was therefore to look after everything, spiritual or profane, and report every detail to the Boss. His independent sources of information [one or two of the nuns who taught in the school at the back of the church and presbytery, the odd parishioner and - soon - the new housekeeper] filled in whatever I may have forgotten, sometimes deliberately, to tell him. Parishioners did so mainly in all innocence. They cheerfully told him how wonderful his new curate was - as all new priests are - or assured him that things ain't what they used to be. I soon got the full grasp of the definition of a curate: *" A mouse training to be a rat"* - by acquiring the art of saying, or at least implying, that there were all kinds of things I would love to do to make life easier for people in the parish but the old man would not allow it!

I could drive a car - so I claimed - but had obviously not had the opportunity at the seminary to take, far less pass, the test. There was a parish Ford which ran well enough but seemed to need nearly as much oil as petrol. Any journey had to be accompanied by a gallon can of oil. This vehicle had hardly been used for two or three years since my predecessor used a very noisy motorbike. My first non-spiritual task was to go out and buy some L plates and then rely on brave or suicidal members of the St. Vincent de Paul Society to accompany me (their shift in the steelworks permitting) on trips around the parish with Holy Communion or expeditions into the countryside to teach children in villages. I also borrowed a bicycle for local work since my vow never to walk again was still in full operation.

It was the custom at that time that on the first Friday of the month innumerable sick and housebound people would want to receive Holy Communion at home. This could quite easily amount to 30 or more, some of whom were genuinely housebound and also would receive the Sacrament every Friday. The additional number was usually accounted for by pious old ladies who somehow could manage to get to Bingo regularly but would hate to miss the First Fridays since they had a firm faith in the miraculous powers of that devotion. [Propagated by St. Margaret Mary Alacoque in the 1670's who was reputedly told in a vision that anyone receiving Holy Communion on nine consecutive first Fridays of the month would be assured of eternal salvation. Although it was not quite as stark and simplistic as was made out it did remain a very worthy devotion.]

My first job would be to say Mass in either the church or the convent and after whatever breakfast I wished to have [cup of coffee and a pipe or - in the weeks after Christmas, often nearly up to Easter] a piece of Christmas cake(s) which were regularly delivered at the festive season to the presbytery, were usually delicious but not touched by anyone but me. Then a pow-wow with the parish priest who may have been fit to have said a Mass or not but was certainly not tempted to do anything more active. I was told what had to be done, how to do it, when and where and when to report back. This kept me going until 1.00 p.m. lunch which was prompt and good and plentiful and never to be missed on pain of instant displeasure.

Monday morning, always, was bank day when the old man was driven (unless prostrate) to the bank with all the cash from the week before and myself as bodyguard and carrier.

There was a lot of copper because of the system of collecting the necessary weekly funds. And, to his credit, he did raise the cash that was required to pay for the schools, the church and presbytery and to allow him to plan future parishes in the town and even to 'endow' them to some extent to give them a good start.

He was good at finances and shrewd in getting loans from the bank or Education Ministry. The debt on the parish was a heavy one and expansion was rampant at that time. But the manner of getting in the cash was the despair of his curates, the envy of other priests and a source of constant wonder to the parishioners.

Chapter V

Our Lady of Walsingham Corby

First there were the Sunday collection(s) and also Holydays of Obligation (and the first thing the Parish Priest did when the new diary appeared was to work out when and if such a holyday would fall on a Sunday. This calamity would mean a loss of income which he would estimate to within an incredibly close amount.) Come rain or shine, summer or winter, people could only enter the church through a side door and get wet and cold if necessary while they paid 'door money' at the table strategically placed to allow only one body in at a time. The heavies who were in charge of the collecting (and the priest who was not saying that Mass usually stood there benignly welcoming the flock) had little piles of small change so that when a 2/6 coin - a half crown - {just over 10p at present} - which was a customary sort of amount - was offered he or she was given back 2/3p. Children were expected to put in a penny or, if getting on a bit, a 3p bit. Clutching their change people then proceeded to spread it through the rest of the collections during Mass: at the Offertory, after Holy Communion and after the Blessing. Should there be a special appeal such as for Foreign Missions or the Diocesan Orphanage, then another and very special collection - often 'lifted' by the priest doing the appealing - would take place after the Consecration. ['Lifted' is the official term for a church collection. You don't 'take it up', collect or gather it. It is lifted!] The wide front doors were then thrown open for people to leave while the new lot waiting for the next Mass were being let in through the side door. [To understand the finances: 6

old pennies were more or less the equivalent now of 2 ½ new pence. There were five such 6 pence's in 'half a crown' or 2/6 and eight half-crowns or 240 pennies in one £1]. I think!

All apparently logical arguments to the effect that just one collection at the door would bring in the same amount and save the bother of giving change were dismissed as having been disproved in practice in the past. Appeals to religion, the liturgy, the importance of prayer during Mass and the reverence due to the sacrament fell on even stonier ground since part of religion and prayer was, in fact, the commandment ' *to contribute to the support of one's pastors'* and thus the Church.

The collections were counted as they came in, still hot from the clutches of the donors. This was done by the priest not saying the Mass and in the old man's room according to a very structured manner with little piles of coins all over the place ready for a final count of the morning's takings before lunch. By then we would know the state of play and the amount would vary somewhat according to the weather or be drastically reduced in the tragic event that a curate was slow in closing the exit doors and some could have come in free rather than pay door money. A catastrophe which any curate would only have allowed to happen once in his career. When evening Mass was introduced this collection was counted before supper so that by Sunday night all was ready for the bank next morning.

Some consideration was given at one point to purchasing a money counting machine as used in banks. Priestly time and zeal, however, was considered far more efficient. Notes were very infrequent and the old pre-decimal coins, we found out, could be separated out with some accuracy by shaking them through a wire 'in-out' office tray so that the smaller coins dropped through and allowed for a certain facility in dealing with the various coins. The highlight of one Sunday count was the finding of a half sovereign - which was promptly reclaimed by an old lady who had put it in by mistake for a farthing - and had the temerity to ring up and tell us so - and then come personally to collect it.

Another great source of income was the Bingo which at that time was all the rage and the Catholic Church had practically a monopoly on it. Every Monday and Thursday we took over the school hall and I trudged off with a suitcase, money bags, tickets and prizes to pretend that I was running this. In fact, the 'callers' were a regular and faithful band of men of the parish who knew exactly what to do and organised the whole thing. I just gave it a veneer of respectability and kept the old man happy. Mondays brought in about Â£100 pure (if one can call it such) profit. Thursday was payday and the place was usually packed. Anything under Â£400 profit was considered a disaster. Two weeks in the year - the last two weeks of July, Glasgow Fair week, their annual holiday - brought in literally thousands of visitors into Corby and the Thursday Bingo was chaotic with every place taken, all the corridors packed and people even sitting in the lavatories listening to the numbers being called on a primitive tannoy we rigged up for the occasion. It was not unusual to make £1000 which I had to carry across a dark playground, late at night, into the presbytery. The men never failed to act as bodyguards but in fact, there was little dread of being mugged. Somehow it never really occurred to any of us that there was such a danger.

I never really understood the niceties of Bingo; how the money was split between prizes and profit, how there were winning lines or combinations other than just the full house and how people could get addicted to the whole thing and develop incredible skill in running up to four or six cards all at the same time. I simply counted money, split up the prizes as instructed and ran the raffle for which I had to buy prizes during the week from various wholesalers and friendly shop keepers. Even in today's money such a profit would be well worth having every week. At that time it was getting on for a fortune.

The next scheme in profitability was the door to door collection every week. 'Volunteers' had a district to cover and a book to keep so that by Thursday night - while I was minting money in the school - the Boss was sitting at home and receiving money collected at 6 pence or a shilling a house. This collection brought in less but gave more aggro since some households did not pay regularly, they were out or broke when called at, collectors failed or forgot and not every book, by any means turned up for the deadline.

Added to this and for the same purpose of paying off the school debt, there was the weekly 'Father's Money' which was expected from every child in the schools on Monday and was collected by the Head Teachers and brought in that afternoon. The expectation there was that every child should bring in at least 3 pence or 6 pence and occasionally the Parish Priest himself went into the schools to boost this racket as the 'Father' in the title.

Finally, twice a year, every district in the parish had an 'At Home' which consisted of a dance and party by the inhabitants of that district; organised by them, catered for by them, attended by them and their friends with donations and a raffle being a '*sine qua non*'; a sort of quadruple whammy inflicted on all the Catholic inhabitants: they gave money, they provided the food, they paid to get in and bought raffle tickets to win prizes they themselves had donated. There were three districts. Those living around the church were the old and established families who were visited by the parish priest and well trained to pay the weekly collection and make the 'At Home' a great success and a bench mark for the rest of the parish. The curates divided the rest of the parish in quite watertight compartments and were blessed with a more mixed population. On arriving in Corby I was given the area around the steelworks at one end of town and the new areas on the other side where a new church would, eventually, be built, plus the outlying villages. On becoming senior curate I also acquired - for a year - all the rest since our Dutch priest, being temporary, was not expected to follow the same pattern. My 'At Homes' in the first year were a source of great distress to the old man since my areas covered the younger families, the more scruffy districts and whole blocks of flats with single men. It also took some time to get to know everybody.

Finally, to raise money and mark social, national and religious highlights in the parish, there were dances in the school hall on the feasts of St. Patrick and St. Andrew usually to the live performance by excellent parish musicians who ran groups specialising in Scottish/Irish dance music rivalling anything on the telly or in the heart of Glasgow or Dublin. An abiding and chilling memory of one St. Patrick's night illustrates the trust one had in one's dog collar and venerable clerical status.

The school hall was packed, the heavy mob of ushers had closed the glass doors in the faces of a contingent of Irish revellers just out of the pubs who were cheerfully banging and kicking on the said doors demanding admission. It looked quite scary when, without a thought (this is how Victoria Crosses are won) I stepped outside and suggested to the rather inebriated mob that they ought to get home, sleep it off and "A Happy St. Patrick's Day to you" but they were too late and the place was full. Grumbling a bit they all calmed down and drifted away. It was only when I saw the terrified faces of the ushers who were getting ready to rush out and rescue me that I realised the folly and danger of what I had done. I was, of course, stone sober but also dressed in full cassock and looking small, young and even innocent.

In addition to all this there was the weekly dance - to recorded music - for teenagers run by the caretaker's wife. This was generally known as 'Nellie's Bin' and we as innocent clergy never darkened the doors of this. In fact, she ruled the kids with a rod of iron and there was never any trouble and certainly no orgies but the picture of teenagers dancing in dim light to modern music (rather than traditional Irish or Scottish) was too daunting for any of us to face. We just took the money.

All this money raising was, truthfully, necessary and it was not wasted. But the effort put into it all, the emphasis on income and - above all - the generosity of the people was truly outstanding. People were not wealthy in the modern sense. Work was plentiful and people worked hard for a good wage in the steelworks. They also spent hard and enjoyed life and did not resent supporting the Church and providing schools for their children. No child was denied a place in a Catholic school and it was a shared pride that we managed to pay our debts and start new parishes, build new churches and schools. Planned giving - by use of envelopes and even an annual and signed promise of donations - was just getting off the ground but the Canon would not even consider it and maintained and even proved that the 'new' system some parishes adopted was not a patch on his system tested by time and illustrated by results.

The Holy Child of Prague statue had pride of place on his mantelpiece. He was convinced that if a silver sixpence lay underneath it then the collections would be maintained, would even improve and the parish would have no financial worries. We curates scoffed at this - discreetly - but were rather shaken when a new housekeeper arrived and removed the coin during a dusting session. The collections diminished dramatically for one week, two weeks and a third. The old man was getting seriously worried; there seemed no rational reason for the decline. One evening he suddenly shot out of his armchair where he was more or less permanently ensconced and lifted up the rather gaudy statue to reveal a blank space! Consternation reigned. A confrontation with the housekeeper revealed the extent of her cleaning activities. A new coin was solemnly substituted, she was strictly admonished never, ever, to touch that coin again and the next week's collections increased equally dramatically to their original total. The curates were impressed, much against their will, and noted all this down for the future and as a lesson from experience.

The housekeeper did not survive all that long after these events. She was one of a line of unfortunate women who had the thankless task of looking after three priests in exchange for a meagre wage plus board and lodging. The lady who had been there when I arrived, whose dog was only just tolerated if he kept out of sight and whose favourite I became because I liked the dog, only stayed a few weeks after my arrival. She retired to live with her maiden sister in Thrapston where I eventually met her again as an aged and slightly embittered parishioner. She was followed by two or three 'daily' housekeepers who did not live in and gave little satisfaction and did not last long. A Bridget with a limp followed but was found to be too decrepit and slap-happy and unwilling to put up with the high expectations of the Parish Priest. Just before her departure a young lady knocked on the door looking for lodgings. I happened to answer the door and gave her an address or two and let her go. The old man - ever fully aware of who was at the door and what was going on - came rushing out, called her back and offered her the job of assistant/trainee housekeeper there and then. No references, no knowledge of her background except for the fact that she had but recently arrived from Ireland.

All went well for two or three weeks until she started feeling unwell in the mornings and even to a bunch of celibates it became clear that the lass was pregnant. The milk of human kindness, hidden somewhere in his bosom, plus our intercession, stopped the old man from following his immediate reaction of packing her off back to Ireland there and then. With not quite indecent haste we did arrange for her to go to a home in Northampton, got in touch with some of her relatives in England and found ourselves, again, at the mercy of a Mrs. Bond who had a heart of gold, the patience of a saint and culinary skill of a derelict cowboy but who was always willing to come in and hold the fort at times of disaster.

A couple was found and became joint housekeepers. Somewhat advanced in years and enjoying a reversal of roles whereby he did the cooking and dusting - with some aplomb - and she mended fuses and did odd jobs with a great show of activity but actually spent most of her time directing her husband's efforts. In a matter of months this arrangement became very burdensome to both sides and a lady in the parish mentioned that she had a younger sister, single, who was a maid in a presbytery in Glasgow.

So we got Edna. Edna was aged about 28 and so below the age (35) recommended by Canon Law as being a safeguard from the temptation of a female housekeeper. She was a simple and willing soul and terrified of the Parish Priest who, in desperation at losing such a succession of housekeepers, pulled out all the stops when she arrived and was charming and encouraging and most generous with his promise of wages, conditions of work and promised time off. None of this increased her confidence much nor did the final promise that for anything she needed in the way of help or advice she could turn to me! In practice, for the next year or so, this meant that I had to check on everything she did which was in any way out of the ordinary, daily housekeeping or cooking. She was confident and capable enough on a day to day basis but anything like a visitor, an extra mouth to feed, a special meal in any way or - God forbid - the visit of the Bishop and she would leave all kinds of things undone in a scientifically haphazard way so that everything - from spoons and an empty salt cellar to the making up of a bed - had to be checked so as to avoid a domestic explosion. Only I was allowed to wipe and put out the crystal glasses and special silver and if a towel was missing in a room or the interval between soup and the main course was too great then it was not just my fault but a deliberate collusion between the two of us.

All this kept Edna in a more or less permanent state of panic in spite of which she was not a bad cook, did do her best and kept the place neat and tidy on the whole as long as the old man was kept out of the kitchen where things were not quite so good and scraps and bits of food tended to be left around in an apparently deliberate act of kindness to germs and, we suspected, even mice and rats. Her habit of serving a fried egg for breakfast with a cigarette dangling from her lips meant that little black bits on the offering were usually taken to be bits of ash and we soon changed to boiled eggs or cornflakes. After parish dances which she was allowed to attend and seemed to enjoy greatly it was not uncommon to have her serving breakfast still in her dancing dress and - as far as one could judge - wearing the same make-up. With lots of covering-up we managed to survive for quite a while, staggering from one crisis to the next. Christmas, however, spelt the death knell of that dubiously domestic bliss.

I was instructed to get a huge turkey so that over the holidays we could simply live off it as and when required. Our butcher provided a real beauty weighing over 30 lbs. On Christmas Day our Edna was invited to eat the festive meal with the three of us. In a state of some stress, after serving and eating the soup, she pushed the turkey through the hatch; the old man produced the carving irons and myself - as senior curate and following the strict hierarchical set-up practised throughout - stood by to pass the plates to those at table. The first slice looked great but when the Canon slipped the knife into the bird to get at the stuffing - lo and behold there was none! Instead, he produced the original plastic bag with the bird's entrails still in it; un-opened, unwashed, raw as received from the butcher. My admiration for his self-control and the grace of the Feast grew mightily as we looked at each other mutely, in awe-struck wonder, knife poised and plate extended. Each of us received just one slice of turkey from the outside - the rest was raw. The turkey never appeared again and Edna's fate was sealed. She left soon after Christmas, given up as a lost cause.

The housekeeper problem was solved by the simple expedient of the old man visiting a priest in what is now the Diocese of East Anglia and, having been wined and dined by his friend, making an offer to his housekeeper which must have been so impressive that she left there and then and came to Corby. And an impressive lady she proved to be. She was a neat and tidy widow with lots of common sense; a marvellous cook and with a fierce loyalty to the Parish Priest from the day she arrived rivalled only by her obvious reluctance to have two curates to look after as well. She did not discriminate in the ordinary things of daily life but made it very clear that curates were there to be tolerated, serve the parish priest and take their proper station in life as God intended. On the whole, however, she made life much more bearable and should be credited with remaining until the old man died and making his last few months comfortable and filled with loving care. She did not need supervision but did tend to become the MI5, secret service and 'enforcer' of the will and wishes of the rightful and all-powerful incumbent.

Chapter V continued

Large though the subject of housekeepers looms in the annals of any parish and the memories of a simple curate at that time there were plenty of other things which are now all part of history. My only experience as a curate was in Corby which was generally acknowledged as being an important parish in the diocese. To begin with, the percentage of Catholics of the total population was way up in the 30% region due to the fact that whole extended families had come from the Glasgow area - true Scots by then but mostly of Irish extraction and, like the many Irish people themselves also there and still coming in, steeped in the traditional Faith of their fathers. It was a young population with marriages and baptisms far more common than funerals. Generally they were ardent in their belief and practice but pugnacious only on one day a year - July 12th.

Orange Day was not a day of civil disorder but friends and neighbours, co-workers, same club members and players in the same football teams marked the day by either marching (if Orange) or scoffing (if not). It shows the innocence and the lack of proper education dished out in the seminary that on the first July 12th of my priestly career, just as I was finishing mid-day Confessions, the sound of fife and drum brought me out in full cassock to stand in front of the church as a motley crew marched past - very slowly - with a brawny character beating hell out of a huge bass drum. This, apparently, was the symbolic 'kicking the Pope' ceremony and my goofy presence was very likely exacerbating the situation and could, according to the irate Parish Priest, have caused a riot. I was whisked out of sight and had the facts of life explained to me. Come July

13th and all was back to normal with Papists and Proddies co-existing peacefully in what was rapidly becoming a very special, unique community of 'Corbyites'.

1960-65 marked, for good or ill, a period of continuity in the parish. The parish priest and two curates were there, unchanged, for five years. Our Dutch priest had left, having done a good job in every way, not least in promoting the devotion to the Sacred Heart and perfecting his English. A newly ordained priest came to fill the post of junior curate and for the next five years we two members of the lowest ranks of the clergy gave each other mutual support, covered up each other's mistakes and aberrations and presented a united front to the 'Old Man'. It also meant that as junior curate he never celebrated a genuine marriage ceremony for years. The 'good' Catholics had a Nuptial Mass celebrated by the parish priest. His assistant as a civilly Authorised Person - me - did all the 'mixed' marriages while the 'convalidations' (of which the least said the better) were done - quietly and with little ceremony - by the civilly unauthorised junior curate. All kinds of other perks/duties/responsibilities sprang from this tight hierarchical set-up but they never interfered with our 'united front' and made no difference to the hard fact: curates were the lowest form of clerical life.

The appointment of a permanent priest meant that my 'district' was much reduced as was the duty of giving instructions to all those happy non-Catholic males who wanted to marry a Catholic girl. These 'mixed marriages' were discouraged but could not, of course, be banned. Non-Catholic young ladies went for their instructions to the sisters in the convent. For a whole year all the men came to me. Most people worked a three shift system in the steelworks so everything else had to adjust. Some pressure was often brought to bear by the Catholic side on the poor swain who was courting their daughter to 'turn' - become a Catholic. This meant keeping to the rule - for ever engraved on my mind - of giving *'at least 24 instructions of at least 40 minutes each lasting at least three months'* before applying to the Bishop for permission to receive the new convert into the Church. Mere pre-nuptial instructions were a lot less but meant that a mixed marriage dispensation had to be applied for (with genuine reasons and safeguards to the faith of the Catholic) and the ceremony itself had to be stark; no Mass, no candles(!), no great celebration. [One of my early clashes with authority was the refusal to ban candles during such weddings. It seemed to be a gratuitous if in itself insignificant insult and eventually the liturgical laws and practices came to be in line with my rebellious attitude!]

At one point I had 27 potential converts under instruction - all individually, weekly and at different times of day according to their shift at work. Plus the simpler forms of preparing non-Catholics for their 'mixed' wedding and, of course, the individual ceremony of receiving converts which was usually a happy occasion attended by all the future in-laws. Some - many - of those thus converted did not, not all that surprisingly, persevere, but quite a few became and continued to be ardent members of the parish. One glowing example was a young Latvian not blessed with many grey brain cells. We took nearly a year and many more than the 24 prescribed sessions before he could even remember that there were seven sacraments and my application for his reception stating that ' he was adequately instructed in the Faith' was very much tongue-in-cheek and fingers crossed. The marriage was gloriously happy and his faith and practice exemplary - as attested to only a year or so ago by his three, now adult children. Presumably, by the law of averages, one had to get something right some time.

[The old man filled in all necessary pre-nuptial forms for all weddings. Questions were to be answered about one's date of birth, baptism, previous (better not be!) marriages, address, parents and any possible relationship, such as first or second cousins, with one's intended. This last question - and this is not in any way apocryphal - was the cause of great mirth and hilarity one evening. The Canon usually asked: "Are you connected?" and on this occasion the bride-to-be blushed prettily and coyly answered: "Only once, Father". He came out of the interview room convulsed with laughter and dined out on this true tale for many a year.]

Curates were appointed or moved more or less at a week's notice according to the will of the Bishop, usually with some discussion with the parish priest but never with actual consultation. They lived in the parish priest's house and obeyed the rules of the establishment with their bed-sit as their only refuge. They received a salary of Â£ 70 a year, their food, drink (preferably non-alcoholic) and lodging were free, and depending on the good will (or not) of the parish priest they received a share of the Christmas and Easter Offerings. They performed their duties as told and in the manner required by the boss. They were entitled to one day off a week plus three Sundays (nearly four weeks if judiciously applied) of annual holidays and were expected to be in the house every night by 11.00 p.m. *'unless charity or parish duties required otherwise'*. They could own a car but only with the grudging and expressed permission of the Bishop.

A surprisingly compassionate touch was the unwritten rule that priests whose families were in Ireland could have a Sunday off after Christmas and after Easter so they could go back to 'the old country' for a reasonably longer visit than just the weekly day off granted to the indigenous low life.

We led a busy but also an ordered, structured life. Each priest had a district for visiting and it was expected that we do this more or less every day, know who was where, who was related to whom, did they attend Sunday Mass, how many children were there and likely to come to our schools etc etc. The first time round was agonising and highly dangerous to the unwary. If a zealous curate asked: " Do you go to Mass?" and the person turned out to be a regular and pious Mass goer then such an enquiry was (quite rightly, when you think of it) regarded as a personal insult and a definite black mark against that priest - to be reported to one's friends and neighbours. After a time one not only got to know the faces of those attending Mass but also read the signs of the not so 'gospel greedy'. If, after being in the place for a few months, a knock on the door did not bring instant recognition and welcome then it was obvious they had not had the privilege of having seen you at the altar. It was unlikely that they attended a church elsewhere; the modern 'voting with your wheels' did not exist at that time. Even the ownership of wheels was limited. If one's visit caused panic (such as the surreptitious stuffing of the 'News of the World' under the couch cushions) it usually signified they meant well but were not all that zealous. If they failed to turn off the TV or even just kept you at the door then there was little hope - I told them my favourite joke and noted them down as 'known but p (for peripheral)' or even as 'l (for lapsed)' in my little black book which had to be guarded with one's life. Loss of it would have meant a lot of extra work plus the danger of blackmail, libel, slander, scandal, possible law suits and certainly an unforgivable breaking of confidentiality.

Mostly, a visit from the priest was very welcome and took place usually midmorning or afternoon. [Attendance at lunch, promptly at 1.00 p.m., was obligatory. Tea at 4.00 p.m. was optional but for absence you were expected to have a good reason. Supper at 7.00 p.m. was mandatory. The food was usually good and plentiful (allowing for housekeeper problems) and the policy was that these young men had to be fed well to keep them healthy and active.] Cups of tea/coffee were always offered (sometimes even a bit of the 'hard stuff') but it was not a good idea to accept too much hospitality; it took too long and raised the spectre of favouritism: If you have a cup at number 8, but not next door, then you are in trouble. Regular visiting was a good way of getting to know people, their lives and hopes and aspirations and often share their problems. Four pennies stacked up on the mantelpiece signified either someone sick in the house or the imminent birth of a baby - private telephones were still the exception but public 'phones were plentiful and usually un-vandalised! The most dangerous pitfall to avoid was to say anything even slightly detrimental, derogatory or critical of anyone else; you were likely to be talking about a distant cousin twice removed who had also moved into Corby from Coatbridge or had been born and bred in the same Irish village.

Two incidents come to mind, both salutary and duly noted for the future. One was of some lady who, very early in my sojourn in Corby, was reported to be going round saying she did not think much of this new curate and did not like him. Since we had never met I found this rather curious and decided to knock on her door and make myself known. A formidable, ginger-haired lady, tall and buxom (or 'carrying all before her' as the Canon used to put it) opened the door and was deflated by my opening remark: "I hear you don't like me". She had no ready answer, I did have a cup of tea (was far too shy to state my preference for coffee, much less insist that it should be stirred anti-clockwise, as I now do) and we parted friends, she probably loved me none the more but accepted the new curate as a necessary evil. Lesson was always to try and find out why one made a bad - or, occasionally, even good - impression.

Another and far more lasting lesson came from a visit to a house where the lady was very pregnant with her first child and I cheerfully said something to the effect that it could well be twins; especially since she had, apparently, a twin sister. In due time one fit and healthy baby was born and the mother seriously and specifically complained to the parish priest that she was very disappointed; I had promised her twins. I was lectured on making flip remarks and making prognostications about something I knew nothing about.

It showed how so many people had - and still have sometimes - a very simple and touching faith in whatever a priest might have said. It gave a great awareness of one's responsibility; how one could affect people for good or bad with innocent but unguarded comments. I never promised anyone twins again and the nearest I got to being involved in a similar but much more happy incident was when I found myself, many years later, feeding one of triplet boys (the father having broken his leg on the day of birth and still being in hospital) and eventually baptising the lot.

The parish priest ran and ruled the parish more or less permanently from his armchair but had all his fingers on the pulse of the establishment, knew everything and everyone and it made our day if we could somehow pull the wool over his eyes, go and be somewhere he did not know or actually present him with something which was 'news'. For a long time we laboured under the illusion that if we went out through the back door he would not know we were actually out. Eventually it became clear that this was not so at all. We worked out the system: he sat in his armchair and kept his door open; the telephone (no extensions except at night) was at his elbow; the mirror above his fireplace reflected the front door and all that happened there; an innocuous landscape picture (not even an Old Master) hanging on the opposite wall reflected the back garden and rear exit. He was the Boss. But usually a benevolent one who did mean well. He was very just and even generous in dividing up the 'income' from personal offerings and had a genuine care for his curates, even if it sometimes became intrusive and smothered any attempt at initiative.

After a dreadful start when he was ill, blamed himself for the disappearance of his senior curate, tried to make sure that it would never happen again by keeping his new curate (me) on a very short leash, found me soft, ignorant, callow, untrained and too submissive - all of which he could only cope with by being, bluntly, a bully and driving me to the verge of a breakdown, I got the best advice of my life from Monsignor (later Bishop) Grant: *"Stand up to him. Swear at him if he swears at you and never give way if you know you are right."* I had an early opportunity to follow this advice on the next Sunday morning when - and how trivial can you get - someone other than the person the Boss had nominated was found selling the Catholic papers at the back of church. I was publicly yelled at and accused of countermanding his orders. I took a deep breath, ignored the by now fascinated worshippers who were making their thanksgiving after Mass, drew myself up to the greatest height I could manage (he was an impressive 6 foot 2 inches) and yelled back telling him that I knew nothing about it, could not care less what arrangements he had made, it had nothing to do with me and I was fed up with being blamed for everything and being shouted at - or words to that effect with at least one 'b' word as far as I remember. The hush in church was awesome but there was no clap of thunder, no shocked voice from heaven. Himself stalked off, I gave a sheepish grin for the benefit of the audience and prepared for the worst when I got back in the house.

Lunch was a quiet meal with the Dutchman, realising something dreadful had happened, trying to make innocent conversation while the old man said not a word and I played the part of a condemned man having his last meal. The incident was not mentioned until after supper when he invited me to his room - and apologised. It was the start of a new era. We still had rows, he was still a grumpy old so and so and looked for faults, criticised, wanted everything done his way, repeatedly made it clear that I was singularly useless, always had been useless and always would be useless. But a certain trust seemed to have sprung up between us which grew - eventually on my part, anyway - into a real affection for him. I could ignore his outbursts, he seemed to accept my failures and shortcomings and, in the long run, he taught me a lot, treated me with justice and showed - when needed - real care and concern. A year or more after my departure when he was dying of cancer and I went to visit him he could still only half-jokingly say, the night before he died, that I was only visiting him because I knew I would be offered a good lunch. And it was, thanks to him, that I was saved from becoming a curate in some other parish in due time and became a 'priest in charge' probably sooner than was normally the custom.

Meanwhile, I had acquired a scooter since getting away to Aylesbury and back on my day off by public transport was impossible and driving the parish car (I had passed my test early in my career) was, apparently, illegal unless it was on 'parish business'. Even getting an old banger was financially impossible and permission would probably have been refused by the bishop - who was no fool and was quite right in claiming that most curates wanted a car to get out of the parish rather than get round it. I got an interest-free loan from the old man himself, bought a Bella scooter in Aylesbury by telephone through a friendly contact, hitchhiked there on my day off [hitchhiking in a dog collar was a doddle], bought some L plates and rode back learning how the thing worked on the way. No crash helmets, no training, no fancy leathers to keep the body together if - when - I fell off, which I did, eventually, some months later, on my way back to Corby late at night.

The whole thing has remained a mystery. I remember leaving home and the rest is a blank until I was - quite tenderly, really, - woken up next morning by the Canon; in my own bed back in Corby. Apparently I had arrived back in the early hours - instead of well before the legal 11.00 p.m. - and it was obvious from scratches on the bike and bruises to myself plus a general goofiness and vagueness well beyond the normal that something untoward had happened. Our good Catholic doctor was called, he put me to bed with a pill and strict instructions to stay there until he checked me over again. The old man served me breakfast in bed and by lunchtime I was pronounced fit and well - but with a permanent memory gap. This caused some concern and was diagnosed as trivial concussion. But for all I knew I might have injured someone, driven over a policeman or robbed a bank. Plus the disconcerting series of small 'faints', lasting only a few seconds, which followed, for no apparent reason, through the next week or so? One was quite spectacular in so far as it happened during Mass in the convent when I blacked out very briefly and woke up shocked and horrified to find myself surrounded by fussing nuns who may well have suspected that I had been at the bottle again. I was sent off to see an expert at St. Crispin's in Duston which at that time was still known as a lunatic asylum! Put into a pair of huge pyjamas I waited in bed for most of the morning while the specialist was delayed because of a blizzard and fallen tress across the road. All I had to read was the front and back of the latest *'News of the World'* which happened to be lying around. Eventually I had some sort of scan which emerged as a graph, was judged to be normal by the expert and I had the evidence presented to me as proof that I was sane. This diagnosis and claim has continued to be disputed by some ever since but the blackouts never occurred again.

I kept the scooter for over a year, paying off my debt with the Christmas and Easter offerings, and then used it as a down payment for an ancient Moggy - the 850 cc gutless wonder with split windscreen, no heater and certainly no radio. [I installed a heater which had two settings: one very cold and the other boiling hot]. With the connivance of the parish priest we did not mention the matter to the bishop which might explain why, a year or so along, when I next sustained a motoring injury I, again, did not even get a day off to recover. This time I was rushing back from Aylesbury to organise a dance in the school hall, hit some ice, turned the car upside down into a ditch, crawled out through the window, walked to the next village, borrowed an old van from the local garage (amazing how trusting total strangers could be when they saw a pathetic and bedraggled figure in clerical garb), drove on to Corby, set up whatever was needed for the dance - and then fainted.

Shock, said the experts. Don't worry but go to Northampton hospital to see about the pain in the back. This I did in yet another, this time borrowed, Morris Minor. An X-ray showed some damage and the result was that I was next hanging - stark naked - from a beam with my toes just touching the ground while two young nurses plastered me from high chest to low hips. I drove back, the plaster dried in the shape of the car seat which was then the only comfortable place for me through the next ten weeks or so. Everything carried on as normal except that I looked a bit tubby, used a long back scratcher to relieve the itch and tended to stand down-wind from people for lack of a bath. On removal of the plaster the back remained tender for a long time and any hope of a career I might have cherished of becoming a weight lifter was shattered.

Before my pride and joy was recovered from the ditch some nasty character had stolen all four wheels. After some weeks I was reunited with the Moggy, eventually part exchanged it for another (a 1000cc one!) and have continued since then being ever in debt for swapped, exchanged, bartered cars; all of which would have been far better if left alone rather than be subjected to my 'improvements' such as air horns, sports carburettors, straight-through exhausts, intricate suspensions, special driving lights, compasses and now GPS navigation systems and speed camera alerts. However, it may be argued that my genuine interest in motoring has been proved by passing the I.A.M. test - twice: once in 1967 and then again in 1982.

Corby did not have a hospital so most urgent sick calls were dealt with by the Kettering clergy. We did, however, have a system for night calls. This was worked out after some friendly discussion so that the doorbell was diverted into the junior curate's room and the telephone was plugged into my room for the night. It was not encouraged to wake the parish priest and we tended to advise people to come and bang on the door or use the telephone - depending on which curate was giving the advice. Night call-outs were not that common but did tend to be interesting. I answered a call at dead of night from an old lady in my district. I knew her as having come from Fort Augustus and having a strong accent which was quite difficult to follow at times. She was quite distraught and said that "Oscar was very poorly". Presuming this to be her son whom I had met briefly I went off into the wilds of a new estate, thumb itching to apply the Holy Oils of the Sacrament of the Sick (then know by the doom-laden name of 'Last Anointing') only to be told that Oscar was her beloved budgie. He did look very poorly even for a budgie in the middle of the night. I blessed him, refrained from 'blessing' her as well, and went back to bed feeling smug and gratified at not being ratty. Next day I went to visit little Oscar and found him fit and chirpy and the old lady grateful and convinced her pet had been saved by my ministrations. Who knows, perhaps he was.

It is a fact that in many cases the Sacrament of the Sick seems to work physical marvels. On one occasion I clearly remember going out in the middle of the night to anoint a man who had had a heart attack at home. The attending doctor did not hold out much hope and did not even call an ambulance. I did my bit and went back to see the family next morning - only to have the patient open the door to me. It may well be that a patient relaxed and improved by knowing that he had made his peace with God and the spirit triumphed over the body. If only people would look at the sacrament as being for the sick; to give them that comfort and peace. Instead, there is still that attitude that it is "the last sacrament" and a priest is called either very late or, even, when a person has already died.

On another night a message came that an Italian worker in the blast furnace had been killed in an accident. Off I rushed to the first aid post there only to be told that he had just left - very dead - in an ambulance to Kettering. Knowing how much it can mean to the family to know that even after death someone dear to them had received the sacrament and reckoning that , since I was already up and about, it would be charitable not to wake the Kettering priests, I raced off to catch the ambulance more or less as it arrived at Kettering hospital - empty. The poor man's body had been deposited in the Corby mortuary situated in a little chapel in the old cemetery. Theological theory and practice dictated that in the case of a sudden death anointing could and should be done, although conditionally, within about three hours. Faithful to my faith and training I went back to Corby police station, ascertained all the facts of the case (a heavy steel beam had fallen and killed the man instantly) and was given the mortuary key and invited to get on with it. At dead of night I stumbled about, could not find any lights but with the aid of my trusty torch (ever being a pessimist in such matters I always have at least one in the car) I slid out several filing cabinets, some empty and some occupied, until one appeared with an Italian name tag on the big toe. Dreading the sight of a mangled body I was greatly relieved to see very little but obviously lethal damage to the head. I anointed his forehead, said a prayer, took the keys back to the police station, had a cup of tea with the duty sergeant and went off to bed with the *gratifying feeling that my duty had been done'* - in the words of Gilbert and Sullivan.

With Sunday and weekday Masses, Benedictions and other services, home Communions and sacraments, instructions of potential converts, visiting, schools, going out to the villages, raising and counting and banking money and innumerable other things such as lengthy Confession sessions, being in charge of a temperamental church heating system (oil fired and with a mind of its own which could be cheated by dangerously 'faking' a pilot light with a taper to make it burst into life), driving the old man around when his cataracts prevented even his suicidal attempts to drive (at times he insisted on crawling along with me as passenger giving him a running commentary on how far he was from the kerb, where the next turn was and the state of oncoming traffic !) not to mention combining forces with my fellow curate as a buffer state between boss and housekeeper, it was a busy life but structured and with clear aims and targets. Changes were coming in the liturgy, Mass attendance was massive and people's need of and use of the Church far greater than it is now. We knew where we stood and what was expected of us and - unless memory plays false - there were far fewer meetings, symposiums or symposia, long-term strategies, discussions and plans. We just got on with things and did them.

Chapter VI

Corby

First there were the Sunday collection(s) and also Holydays of Obligation (and the first thing the Parish Priest did when the new diary appeared was to work out when and if such a holyday would fall on a Sunday. This calamity would mean a loss of income which he would estimate to within an incredibly close amount.) Come rain or shine, summer or winter, people could only enter the church through a side door and get wet and cold if necessary while they paid 'door money' at the table strategically placed to allow only one body in at a time. The heavies who were in charge of the collecting (and the priest who was not saying that Mass usually stood there benignly welcoming the flock) had little piles of small change so that when a 2/6 coin - a half crown - {just over 10p at present} - which was a customary sort of amount - was offered he or she was given back 2/3p. Children were expected to put in a penny or, if getting on a bit, a 3p bit. Clutching their change people then proceeded to spread it through the rest of the collections during Mass: at the Offertory, after Holy Communion and after the Blessing. Should there be a special appeal such as for Foreign Missions or the Diocesan Orphanage, then another and very special collection - often 'lifted' by the priest doing the appealing - would take place after the Consecration. ['Lifted' is the official term for a church collection. You don't 'take it up', collect or gather it. It is lifted!] The wide front doors were then thrown open for people to leave while the new lot waiting for the next Mass were being let in through the side door. [To understand the finances: 6 old pennies were more or less the equivalent now of 2 ½ new pence. There were five such 6 pence's in 'half a crown' or 2/6 and eight half-crowns or 240 pennies in one £1]. I think!

All apparently logical arguments to the effect that just one collection at the door would bring in the same amount and save the bother of giving change were dismissed as having been disproved in practice in the past. Appeals to religion, the liturgy, the importance of prayer during Mass and the reverence due to the sacrament fell on even stonier ground since part of religion and prayer was, in fact, the commandment ' *to contribute to the support of one's pastors'* and thus the Church.

The collections were counted as they came in, still hot from the clutches of the donors. This was done by the priest not saying the Mass and in the old man's room according to a very structured manner with little piles of coins all over the place ready for a final count of the morning's takings before lunch. By then we would know the state of play and the amount would vary somewhat according to the weather or be drastically reduced in the tragic event that a curate was slow in closing the exit doors and some could have come in free rather than pay door money. A catastrophe which any curate would only have allowed to happen once in his career. When evening Mass was introduced this collection was counted before supper so that by Sunday night all was ready for the bank next morning.

Some consideration was given at one point to purchasing a money counting machine as used in banks. Priestly time and zeal, however, was considered far more efficient. Notes were very infrequent and the old pre-decimal coins, we found out, could be separated out with some accuracy by shaking them through a wire 'in-out' office tray so that the smaller coins dropped through and allowed for a certain facility in dealing with the various coins. The highlight of one Sunday count was the finding of a half sovereign - which was promptly reclaimed by an old lady who had put it in by mistake for a farthing - and had the temerity to ring up and tell us so - and then come personally to collect it.

Another great source of income was the Bingo which at that time was all the rage and the Catholic Church had practically a monopoly on it. Every Monday and Thursday we took over the school hall and I trudged off with a suitcase, money bags, tickets and prizes to pretend that I was running this. In fact, the 'callers' were a regular and faithful band of men of the parish who knew exactly what to do and organised the whole thing. I just gave it a veneer of respectability and kept the old man happy. Mondays brought in about Â£100 pure (if one can call it such) profit. Thursday was payday and the place was usually packed. Anything under Â£400 profit was considered a disaster. Two weeks in the year - the last two weeks of July, Glasgow Fair week, their annual holiday - brought in literally thousands of visitors into Corby and the Thursday Bingo was chaotic with every place taken, all the corridors packed and people even sitting in the lavatories listening to the numbers being called on a primitive tannoy we rigged up for the occasion. It was not unusual to make £1000 which I had to carry across a dark playground, late at night, into the presbytery. The men never failed to act as bodyguards but in fact, there was little dread of being mugged. Somehow it never really occurred to any of us that there was such a danger.

I never really understood the niceties of Bingo; how the money was split between prizes and profit, how there were winning lines or combinations other than just the full house and how people could get addicted to the whole thing and develop incredible skill in running up to four or six cards all at the same time. I simply counted money, split up the prizes as instructed and ran the raffle for which I had to buy prizes during the week from various wholesalers and friendly shop keepers. Even in today's money such a profit would be well worth having every week. At that time it was getting on for a fortune.

The next scheme in profitability was the door to door collection every week. 'Volunteers' had a district to cover and a book to keep so that by Thursday night - while I was minting money in the school - the Boss was sitting at home and receiving money collected at 6 pence or a shilling a house. This collection brought in less but gave more aggro since some households did not pay regularly, they were out or broke when called at, collectors failed or forgot and not every book, by any means turned up for the deadline.

Added to this and for the same purpose of paying off the school debt, there was the weekly 'Father's Money' which was expected from every child in the schools on Monday and was collected by the Head Teachers and brought in that afternoon. The expectation there was that every child should bring in at least 3 pence or 6 pence and occasionally the Parish Priest himself went into the schools to boost this racket as the 'Father' in the title.

Finally, twice a year, every district in the parish had an 'At Home' which consisted of a dance and party by the inhabitants of that district; organised by them, catered for by them, attended by them and their friends with donations and a raffle being a '*sine qua non*'; a sort of quadruple whammy inflicted on all the Catholic inhabitants: they gave money, they provided the food, they paid to get in and bought raffle tickets to win prizes they themselves had donated. There were three districts. Those living around the church were the old and established families who were visited by the parish priest and well trained to pay the weekly collection and make the 'At Home' a great success and a bench mark for the rest of the parish. The curates divided the rest of the parish in quite watertight compartments and were blessed with a more mixed population. On arriving in Corby I was given the area around the steelworks at one end of town and the new areas on the other side where a new church would, eventually, be built, plus the outlying villages. On becoming senior curate I also acquired - for a year - all the rest since our Dutch priest, being temporary, was not expected to follow the same pattern. My 'At Homes' in the first year were a source of great distress to the old man since my areas covered the younger families, the more scruffy districts and whole blocks of flats with single men. It also took some time to get to know everybody.

Finally, to raise money and mark social, national and religious highlights in the parish, there were dances in the school hall on the feasts of St. Patrick and St. Andrew usually to the live performance by excellent parish musicians who ran groups specialising in Scottish/Irish dance music rivalling anything on the telly or in the heart of Glasgow or Dublin. An abiding and chilling memory of one St. Patrick's night illustrates the trust one had in one's dog collar and venerable clerical status.

The school hall was packed, the heavy mob of ushers had closed the glass doors in the faces of a contingent of Irish revellers just out of the pubs who were cheerfully banging and kicking on the said doors demanding admission. It looked quite scary when, without a thought (this is how Victoria Crosses are won) I stepped outside and suggested to the rather inebriated mob that they ought to get home, sleep it off and "A Happy St. Patrick's Day to you" but they were too late and the place was full. Grumbling a bit they all calmed down and drifted away. It was only when I saw the terrified faces of the ushers who were getting ready to rush out and rescue me that I realised the folly and danger of what I had done. I was, of course, stone sober but also dressed in full cassock and looking small, young and even innocent.

In addition to all this there was the weekly dance - to recorded music - for teenagers run by the caretaker's wife. This was generally known as 'Nellie's Bin' and we as innocent clergy never darkened the doors of this. In fact, she ruled the kids with a rod of iron and there was never any trouble and certainly no orgies but the picture of teenagers dancing in dim light to modern music (rather than traditional Irish or Scottish) was too daunting for any of us to face. We just took the money.

All this money raising was, truthfully, necessary and it was not wasted. But the effort put into it all, the emphasis on income and - above all - the generosity of the people was truly outstanding. People were not wealthy in the modern sense. Work was plentiful and people worked hard for a good wage in the steelworks. They also spent hard and enjoyed life and did not resent supporting the Church and providing schools for their children. No child was denied a place in a Catholic school and it was a shared pride that we managed to pay our debts and start new parishes, build new churches and schools. Planned giving - by use of envelopes and even an annual and signed promise of donations - was just getting off the ground but the Canon would not even consider it and maintained and even proved that the 'new' system some parishes adopted was not a patch on his system tested by time and illustrated by results.

The Holy Child of Prague statue had pride of place on his mantelpiece. He was convinced that if a silver sixpence lay underneath it then the collections would be maintained, would even improve and the parish would have no financial worries. We curates scoffed at this - discreetly - but were rather shaken when a new housekeeper arrived and removed the coin during a dusting session. The collections diminished dramatically for one week, two weeks and a third. The old man was getting seriously worried; there seemed no rational reason for the decline. One evening he suddenly shot out of his armchair where he was more or less permanently ensconced and lifted up the rather gaudy statue to reveal a blank space! Consternation reigned. A confrontation with the housekeeper revealed the extent of her cleaning activities. A new coin was solemnly substituted, she was strictly admonished never, ever, to touch that coin again and the next week's collections increased equally dramatically to their original total. The curates were impressed, much against their will, and noted all this down for the future and as a lesson from experience.

The housekeeper did not survive all that long after these events. She was one of a line of unfortunate women who had the thankless task of looking after three priests in exchange for a meagre wage plus board and lodging. The lady who had been there when I arrived, whose dog was only just tolerated if he kept out of sight and whose favourite I became because I liked the dog, only stayed a few weeks after my arrival. She retired to live with her maiden sister in Thrapston where I eventually met her again as an aged and slightly embittered parishioner. She was followed by two or three 'daily' housekeepers who did not live in and gave little satisfaction and did not last long. A Bridget with a limp followed but was found to be too decrepit and slap-happy and unwilling to put up with the high expectations of the Parish Priest. Just before her departure a young lady knocked on the door looking for lodgings. I happened to answer the door and gave her an address or two and let her go. The old man - ever fully aware of who was at the door and what was going on - came rushing out, called her back and offered her the job of assistant/trainee housekeeper there and then. No references, no knowledge of her background except for the fact that she had but recently arrived from Ireland.

All went well for two or three weeks until she started feeling unwell in the mornings and even to a bunch of celibates it became clear that the lass was pregnant. The milk of human kindness, hidden somewhere in his bosom, plus our intercession, stopped the old man from following his immediate reaction of packing her off back to Ireland there and then. With not quite indecent haste we did arrange for her to go to a home in Northampton, got in touch with some of her relatives in England and found ourselves, again, at the mercy of a Mrs. Bond who had a heart of gold, the patience of a saint and culinary skill of a derelict cowboy but who was always willing to come in and hold the fort at times of disaster.

A couple was found and became joint housekeepers. Somewhat advanced in years and enjoying a reversal of roles whereby he did the cooking and dusting - with some aplomb - and she mended fuses and did odd jobs with a great show of activity but actually spent most of her time directing her husband's efforts. In a matter of months this arrangement became very burdensome to both sides and a lady in the parish mentioned that she had a younger sister, single, who was a maid in a presbytery in Glasgow.

So we got Edna. Edna was aged about 28 and so below the age (35) recommended by Canon Law as being a safeguard from the temptation of a female housekeeper. She was a simple and willing soul and terrified of the Parish Priest who, in desperation at losing such a succession of housekeepers, pulled out all the stops when she arrived and was charming and encouraging and most generous with his promise of wages, conditions of work and promised time off. None of this increased her confidence much nor did the final promise that for anything she needed in the way of help or advice she could turn to me! In practice, for the next year or so, this meant that I had to check on everything she did which was in any way out of the ordinary, daily housekeeping or cooking. She was confident and capable enough on a day to day basis but anything like a visitor, an extra mouth to feed, a special meal in any way or - God forbid - the visit of the Bishop and she would leave all kinds of things undone in a scientifically haphazard way so that everything - from spoons and an empty salt cellar to the making up of a bed - had to be checked so as to avoid a domestic explosion. Only I was allowed to wipe and put out the crystal glasses and special silver and if a towel was missing in a room or the interval between soup and the main course was too great then it was not just my fault but a deliberate collusion between the two of us.

All this kept Edna in a more or less permanent state of panic in spite of which she was not a bad cook, did do her best and kept the place neat and tidy on the whole as long as the old man was kept out of the kitchen where things were not quite so good and scraps and bits of food tended to be left around in an apparently deliberate act of kindness to germs and, we suspected, even mice and rats. Her habit of serving a fried egg for breakfast with a cigarette dangling from her lips meant that little black bits on the offering were usually taken to be bits of ash and we soon changed to boiled eggs or cornflakes. After parish dances which she was allowed to attend and seemed to enjoy greatly it was not uncommon to have her serving breakfast still in her dancing dress and - as far as one could judge - wearing the same make-up. With lots of covering-up we managed to survive for quite a while, staggering from one crisis to the next. Christmas, however, spelt the death knell of that dubiously domestic bliss.

I was instructed to get a huge turkey so that over the holidays we could simply live off it as and when required. Our butcher provided a real beauty weighing over 30 lbs. On Christmas Day our Edna was invited to eat the festive meal with the three of us. In a state of some stress, after serving and eating the soup, she pushed the turkey through the hatch; the old man produced the carving irons and myself - as senior curate and following the strict hierarchical set-up practised throughout - stood by to pass the plates to those at table. The first slice looked great but when the Canon slipped the knife into the bird to get at the stuffing - lo and behold there was none! Instead, he produced the original plastic bag with the bird's entrails still in it; un-opened, unwashed, raw as received from the butcher. My admiration for his self-control and the grace of the Feast grew mightily as we looked at each other mutely, in awe-struck wonder, knife poised and plate extended. Each of us received just one slice of turkey from the outside - the rest was raw. The turkey never appeared again and Edna's fate was sealed. She left soon after Christmas, given up as a lost cause.

The housekeeper problem was solved by the simple expedient of the old man visiting a priest in what is now the Diocese of East Anglia and, having been wined and dined by his friend, making an offer to his housekeeper which must have been so impressive that she left there and then and came to Corby. And an impressive lady she proved to be. She was a neat and tidy widow with lots of common sense; a marvellous cook and with a fierce loyalty to the Parish Priest from the day she arrived rivalled only by her obvious reluctance to have two curates to look after as well. She did not discriminate in the ordinary things of daily life but made it very clear that curates were there to be tolerated, serve the parish priest and take their proper station in life as God intended. On the whole, however, she made life much more bearable and should be credited with remaining until the old man died and making his last few months comfortable and filled with loving care. She did not need supervision but did tend to become the MI5, secret service and 'enforcer' of the will and wishes of the rightful and all-powerful incumbent.

Chapter VII

St Pauls Thrapston

February 1965 brought a memorable day. I reached the age of 30.

"So what" you might well say. "It happens to lots of people". However, during my undistinguished career at the boarding school in Buckingham a holy Franciscan priest, for reasons known only to himself, had formally and publicly told me that I would be dead before the age of 30. This prophecy did not really loom over my youth, but I did remember it and had mentioned it to my fellow clergy - who touchingly opened a celebratory bottle at lunch to mark the fallibility of prophets.

The time was, however, approaching when my curacy in Corby ought to come to an end. If a man was moved too often and regularly then it augured badly for his future since the inherited wisdom was that a bad curate would make a bad parish priest. If he stayed for too long then the suspicion was that nobody else wanted him. Five or six years seemed to be the norm and it so happened that just at this time a diocesan priest was retiring as chaplain to the forces after a 20 year stint. The unwritten law was that the diocese would have to replace him and there happened to be a vacancy in the RAF.

I volunteered. It seemed a good idea at the time and I did have links to the Air Force through my father. With the knowledge of my parish priest and the blessing of the Vicar General - Mgr Charles Grant, soon to become auxiliary bishop - I went for an interview at Adastral House in London. The senior Catholic Chaplain - a Mgr. Roche towering over me at some six foot six - went through my short sacerdotal history, treated me to a good lunch and declared himself willing to have me appointed - subject to a medical and the written permission of my bishop. The medical for a chaplain, it seems, was just to confirm officially that he was breathing. Permission from the Bishop, it was presumed, was there since the Vicar General knew all about it.

The Bishop did not, however. Mgr. Grant, - in his accustomed gentle and laid-back manner - had never thought to mention such a trivial event. The first the Bishop knew about it was at some funeral in Birmingham when the Bishop of the Forces - rejoicing in the name of Mgr. Tickle - cheerfully said to him that he would have this young chap from his Diocese and thanks for sending someone. I was summoned to appear on the Episcopal carpet and he read the riot act, accusing me of doing things behind his back, being ungrateful to the diocese which had accepted me, neglecting my duty to the parish and the schools, letting down my parish priest not to mention the dignity of my bishop. Unfrocking in the middle of winter seemed a distinct possibility until the bishop had to draw breath and I pointed out that I had done everything by the book - permission and blessing of Vicar General, agreement of parish priest etc.

He telephoned Mgr. Grant there and then, listened, calmed down and even apologised - but made it clear that my future duties lay in looking after schools (my job was simply to act as secretary - or 'correspondent' as the official description had it - to several boards of Governors chaired by the old man and I was the only handy curate who could type with four fingers rather than the usual two) and there was no way I was going to go off to be a chaplain - even just for the suggested four years. I had no problem accepting his decision; I had not set my mind on anything and also realised that they were shooting British servicemen in Cyprus and other trouble spots. Another priest was sent off to do a four year term. He did not really want to go but accepted the appointment, enjoyed his time in the RAF and got back safely without being shot.

[Just a few words of wonder and appreciation of old Bishop Leo Parker who was appointed in 1941 and ruled the diocese in an autocratic but usually benevolent and patriarchal manner for more than a quarter of a century. His motto: "Deus Providebit" - God will provide - did sometimes also include the next word from its scriptural context: "a victim", but he was in full charge of six counties stretching from Slough right up to Norwich and encompassing all those lovely little parishes along the east coast where we all wished to retire in the long run to play golf, walk a dog and have peace and quiet. He travelled huge distances (during the war without benefit of road sign posts) and knew every priest and every church. With his priest secretary he dealt with all correspondence (more often than not in his very own handwriting with its characteristic slant upwards from left to right), all permissions, dispensations, notifications and diocesan propaganda. The diocesan treasury and treasurer consisted of one man - for years Canon Hunting - who was also in charge of the orphanage(s). Someone, some time, really ought to add up the number of churches and schools old Leo blessed and opened during that period when the Church was growing and flourishing and the diocese had to cope with an influx of immigrants and a great exodus from London. He also had his quaint foibles and rigid rules. Quite often using the royal "we" his official visitations of parishes were thorough and left few stones unturned. I was called down into the old man's study at one visitation to find the bishop sitting comfortably in the sacred armchair vacated for the occasion, a whisky at his elbow, perusing the Baptismal Register and wanting to know, quite mildly: " Since when, Father, have you been a Bishop?" Flummoxed by this approach and resisting the temptation to make the flippant reply that this would be a fate worse than death I was saved from doing myself further damage by having it pointed out that in one entry I had signed using my Christian name only - a privilege exclusively reserved to bishops. It was rumoured that until he found something amiss he would be on edge and that a wily parish priest solved this problem by placing a

rocking horse in the entrance hall to the presbytery. The sight of this so threw the bishop that he spent the whole week-end happy and trying to find out what the thing was doing there. A custom he also initiated was to have a diocesan Deacon assist at Midnight Mass and the solemn Christmas Day Mass in the Cathedral. [There was no such thing at that time as a 'Permanent Deacon'. The Diaconate was simply what followed the sub-diaconate - logically enough - and led up to the Priesthood.] In 1958 I was summoned to perform this duty, sent a postal order for £5 as travelling expenses and ordered to present myself at Bishop's House in plenty of time. The Rector of the seminary was not pleased since it was customary for us to remain there until the Feast of St. John on December 27th. I had my orders, he was a mere Mgr, not a Bishop, so I travelled by bus on Christmas Eve, mugged up the liturgical details of a Deacon's function at High Masses and presented myself at Bishop's House to be shown into a guest room by one of the severe-looking nuns who ran the household. It was freezing, I was not offered supper but did perform perfectly my midnight function in a beautiful and solemn Mass. I sang the Gospel in Latin like a nightingale and the dismissal with a flourish worthy of a Caruso. No refreshments followed since one had to fast from midnight and on jumping into bed I nearly broke my toe on a stone hot water bottle a charitable nun had put between the sheets. Next morning's Mass was equally solemn and packed and was followed by the offer of a glass of whisky and a piece of pork pie. Too hungry and intimidated to refuse either I was packed and ready to depart by 1.00 p.m. There were no trains, no buses on Christmas Day and traffic in general at that time was sparse in comparison to our present ever threatening gridlock. I stood along Barrack Road in Northampton in full clericals with thumb outstretched to be picked up within minutes by a Rolls Royce whose elderly driver was, I am still convinced, an angel in disguise. A very good disguise since he was an elderly gentleman who, once he had fathomed out the mystery of a priest (the subtle difference between a deacon and a 'padre' evaded him) hitch *hiking on Christmas Day, hardly said another word but not only took me to Aylesbury but actually dropped me at my mother's door. It was my first trip in a Roller and probably the next one will be in a hearse - although they are now tending to use custom-made Fords. The rest of Christmas Day was spent at home, the first for five years or so, and on Boxing Day I had to rely on the Green Line bus services to take me back to Wonersh to celebrate the patronal feast. (It goes to show how rigid the seminary rules still were: I was only allowed out for the minimum of time to assist in the Cathedral but had to be back for the 27th even though we all started the Christmas holidays on the 28th. Bishop Parker retired in 1967 and has left an indelible mark on this Diocese - just look at the foundation stones of churches and schools and ask any priest who is getting on a bit for more anecdotes of the 'good old days'.]*

A collection of Father Stan's Pipes kept in his caravan in Thrapston

The Canon prided himself, with some justification, on not only training (or breaking in) his 'boys' but also setting them up in a parish when it was time to leave. Both my predecessors had progressed to taking over a new parish in Corby. My apparently indispensable role in the schools plus a certain influence the old man seemed to have with the bishop meant that I was, after six years, promoted to be 'Priest in Charge' of Thrapston, a small town some 10 miles away which had a new church but no living quarters. This was duly published in the normal diocesan and national media as being quite a separate appointment than that of a mere curate but meant that I would actually live in Wellingborough with the parish priest there, Fr. Ethelbert Payne.

He was a lovely, gentle priest in his mid-sixties who had a very personal and fatherly relationship with his parishioners and the last thing he wanted was a curate to share this happy state. He welcomed me warmly, fed and lodged me generously, shared his classical records with me and even welcomed my newly acquired dog - Butch - into his household. He made it very clear, however, that my contribution to the parish was to be quite limited - one Sunday Mass and full responsibility for the Borstal - a division of labour which made him happy and gave me plenty of time to get involved out in the wilds of my new 'parish' which consisted of Thrapston plus about 25 villages.

I loved the pleasant and casual arrangement but hated that Borstal. Needless to say, I was installed as chaplain with no training, warning or preparation. The system has now been long abolished but it was an establishment - in this case a strict one only just below the strictest of all at some place at Feltwell which was only spoken of in whispers and where everything had to be done 'at the double' - for young males between the ages of 18 and 21 who had in some way or another fallen foul of the law. It was stressed that it was not a punishment but a period of training of no fixed length but no less than six months and no more than three years and that good behaviour and progress in 'training' affected the release or otherwise of the inmates. These varied in the gravity of their offences and ranged from some unfortunates who had merely found themselves in broken homes, been sent 'into care', moved up to approved schools and detention centres and had done nothing worse than abscond and possibly pilfered from shops to keep alive, to hardened dope pushers, car thieves, rapists and one or two murderers - one of whom was a Catholic public school boy who, at the age of 15, had slit his fosterfather's throat with a razor and was being detained 'at Her Majesty's Pleasure'. The one common factor seemed to be that the recidivist record was sky high - some 85% of inmates graduated, sooner or later, to become inmates in a genuine prison.

All being under the age of 21 they were obliged to state their religion, were entitled to benefit from the services of a minister and - in the case of Roman Catholics - also obliged to attend a weekly act of worship. Ideally this should have been on a Sunday but a clash of parish Masses and institution time-table meant that the weekly Mass had to be fixed for a Tuesday - at 6.30 a.m.! [I continued my classical music education by listening to Radio 3 on the way to this weekly celebration.] The job also entailed at least two visits every week to meet newcomers - help to induct them into the mysteries of this institution - and deal with any requests to me 'the padre' - who duly attended, chained to a key which opened all doors and had to be safeguarded with one's life. [A salutary warning happened early on in my prison career when the Methodist minister lost his key and all the locks had to be changed at great expense and to the lasting disgrace of the unfortunate minister.]

Right from the start there was a spectacular increase in the number of 'lads' (as they were officially called) who claimed to be R.C's. Mass attendance on a Tuesday boomed and there was a great demand for Catholic Bibles. My original pleasant surprise quickly deteriorated into stark realism and even cynicism.

The thin pages from the Bible were, the Warden told me, ideal for rolling 'snouts' or cigarettes - but I was welcome to requisition for as many as I thought I needed. Mass attendance on a Tuesday at that ungodly hour meant that the R.C's lined up and marched down to chapel and did not have to do the daily 'slopping out'; it was done by the remaining heretical members of the establishment. The Bible situation was resolved and demand plummeted by offering separate books of the Old and New Testament with hard covers and thick pages. The Mass time was changed to 7.00 a.m. and attendance dropped to something around 20% of inhabitants of genuine, baptised Catholics. (Still more - and this was general among the prison population - than the national 10% to 12% average. No doubt students of criminology have an answer to this anomaly.) Slopping out on Tuesdays ceased to be reserved for heretics but Catholics on that morning were deprived of some of their free or 'association' time. Not the most popular change their new chaplain initiated.

Making Mass obligatory did nothing to make it sacred or devout. Some 25 to 30 lads were herded into the chapel and the 'screws' kept good order and discipline. Only a few gave responses or even signs of awareness. To my lasting shame and continued embarrassment I once insisted on saying the 'Our Father' in the Mass five or six times until the whole congregation joined in. Eventually they all did, but it was an abuse of power, verging on blasphemy and certainly defeated the whole purpose of prayer and devotion. My visits, as really the whole principle and set-up of Borstal training, were usually quite ineffective. Few were really interested in 'religion' of any sort or at any level and mostly looked on the chaplain as a 'soft touch' to be used for getting perks. I soon learned to leave my tobacco pouch in the car so I could honestly say I had no 'makings' on me for a quick smoke. On a few occasions I was able to give some encouragement or consolation but the rules were strict and relentless and aimed at making all equal, subservient and, as far as possible, broken in spirit.

One case stands out as tragic and myself utterly useless. A young lad with only a moderate and non-violent criminal record and a reasonably amiable disposition was informed that his and his girlfriend's baby had just been stillborn. He was frantic with genuine grief and concern and we requested permission for him to attend the funeral. This was refused at local level and the appeal to the Home Office confirmed this. I volunteered, probably foolishly and in writing, to go with him, be handcuffed to him and guarantee his safe return. A bowler-hatted gentleman from H.Q. came especially to see me, point out the danger and the worthlessness of such a guarantee and advised me - for the good of any future hopes I might have in the Prison Service - to drop the matter. I had, certainly by then, no hopes or aspirations in that Service but could not appeal to any higher authority, the funeral had taken place and the lad was moved to another, like but not worse, institution. The reason for refusal was simply that it would have created a precedent and that I was acting beyond my brief. The Warden, to his credit, was sympathetic but equally powerless.

My three years or so serving this Borstal were undistinguished, pointless and unhappy. Fortunately the whole system was soon to be discontinued but not really replaced by anything better. The training given was minimal and the place was really just a school for crime where most lads graduated with a first class degree. Even I learnt how to transfer signatures from one cheque to another by the use of a raw potato, how to start a car without an ignition key and, of course, how useful Bible pages could be to smokers.

The rest of my first 18 months or so of being a 'priest in charge' were happy and very busy. I was comfortably based in Wellingborough but spent most of my time in Thrapston and getting to know and be known in the surrounding villages. There had not been a resident priest for many years. The district had originally been served by Dominican priests from Laxton who celebrated a regular Sunday Mass in a small wooden hall in the middle of an allotment. [The piece of land had been donated by the 'Father' of the parish, a gem of a gentleman who, with his sister, had become Catholics. Bishop Parker, on being asked for permission to put up a hut because there were at least two Catholics in the town, was reputed to have said - obviously not knowing all the details - " Good. Let them get married and start a dynasty"] Then the priest from Oundle took over and for five or six years previous to my august appointment the place was an offshoot and definitely sideline from Wellingborough. A faithful core of Catholics kept the Faith alive but most villages had never see a Catholic priest in the flesh for ages. There was a lovely new church with half an acre of land but no living quarters. There was, however, a comfortable bed in the sacristy, artfully designed to hinge into invisibility in the wall, where I could stay if too tired or bone idle to return to Wellingborough I inherited a book with some addresses. One particular character had his name underlined in red and a caution had been added, also in red: 'Avoid this man. He is a blasphemer.' I promptly went to visit him and found a charming old gentleman who had spent years in India as a tea planter. He never went to Mass - seldom left the house - and had an endless store of fascinating stories of the days of the British Empire which he was fond of telling and generously peppered with expletives (not deleted, as President Nixon's were reputed to be). His theological views were suspect, to say the least, but he had his own belief in his own God and in due time I gave him a simple burial according to his wishes and have every confidence that God welcomed him, warts and all.

Generally, however, it was a matter of finding out who the Catholics were and where in the scattered countryside they lived. I developed this search into a fine art, having picked the brains of all known Catholics I then systematically and slowly visited every village and hamlet. In those days most had a Post Office and shop. A visit to this and the purchase of a stamp or ounce of tobacco, flaunting the clerical collar and usually stroking the resident dog or cat was a sure opener to a conversation with the postmaster/usually mistress. Their knowledge was invariably encyclopaedic with intimate family details of the local inhabitants thrown in for free. A call at the door of known or suspected Catholics was then the start of a link - or not.

Knowledge thus gleaned was then confirmed and added to by a visit to the local public house (no village was without at least one) and the slow consumption of a half pint of local ale. A few eyebrows rose at the vision of a little cleric with a big dog standing at the bar but the natives were practically always friendly and more than willing to point out possible candidates for a visit. All this took time and the purchase of a stamp or tobacco was blameless enough but drinking more than half a pint in more than one pub per day could have had dire consequences - for one's ability to drive and general reputation, nor were visits always welcome and one's informant or grass had to be kept confidential. Gradually, however, it became known that there was a local Catholic priest who was harmless, definitely a bit odd but liked animals, helped people on the road when their vehicle broke down [my first notorious exploit and the start of 35 years of friendship with the stranded victim was in the middle of a severe winter when I towed an electric milkfloat - which had run out of juice- up a very steep hill, back to its socket and source of power. On another occasion on the same hill I managed to tow a minibus on its way to a children's nursery. Again, present laws did not apply and the 12 seater was packed with well over 20 assorted infants who then gave me a song when we safely arrived at our destination.] and was more than willing to talk football, farming, listen patiently to fishermen's tall tales and did not insist on ramming religion down their throats. I was always recognisable by wearing black and the clerical collar and encouraged the children to believe that I slept in black pyjamas as well and - even then - gave them lollies.

All was gradually developing into a comfortable rut - with the Borstal the only fly in the ointment - with comfortable lodgings in Wellingborough and regular trips and square meals in Corby doing my cushy school jobs when Fr. Payne went off in August 1967 for a week's holiday on the Isle of Wight. He died there quite unexpectedly of a massive heart attack to the great sorrow of all his friends and parishioners. Both he and the Canon (who died in November of the same year) had, in very different ways, become father figures to me as well as friends and sources of help and good advice. I missed them both and their deaths marked a great change in the character of both parishes. In Corby it was the end of that five or six year period of stability with a new parish priest and a succession and rapid turnover of curates with a reduction quite soon to only one assistant.

In Wellingborough the death of Bert Payne, as he was affectionately known, was to some extent opportune - for him. The place was exploding with the development of industry and new housing and desperately needed a full time curate; which would have made old Bert quite unhappy. He was already beginning to realise that his gentle, individual and paternal approach was not going to be able to cope with the growing numbers in his parish. A week or so before his holiday and death we had, quite coincidentally, been talking about making a will and I was quite sure that he had said that he had made his sometime before and it was in his room. After the funeral his brother and I went through all the effects repeatedly and never found any kind of will. Eventually his brother took the car and the imposing stereo system but left everything else to be disposed of in whatever way I might choose. It was rather sad. His clothes did not fit me (I was still slim and handsome at the time), his books were distributed among his friends and parishioners, I kept most of his classical LP records (and had them still up to a year or so ago. They were immaculate, only handled by him with white gloves and kept fastidiously in their proper jackets) while whole shelves of nick-knacks and mementoes brought to him by parishioners (especially children) from holidays and pilgrimages found their forlorn way into jumble sales. He had spent quite a few years in Wellingborough, loved it and its people and would have been very unhappy at the rapid changes in the next year or so.

The next three or four months were a bit chaotic. I was in charge of Wellingborough and Thrapston and was sent a priest just returned from the States from a religious order. He was a most gentle, kind and conscientious priest but with no initiative whatever and so timid that it was a mystery how he survived. I was not used to having, in effect, a curate and forgot in the first few weeks even to suggest that he should take a day off - or provide him with any money. Whatever he was asked to do he did willingly and faithfully and well but I could not bring myself to throw him to the lions in the Borstal. It was impossible not to get on well with him but I was not used to being paternal and fear that at times he must have found me uncaring and not sufficiently supportive.

A new parish priest, full of energy and ideas very different to old Bert's, was duly appointed, our temporary assistant left to help out in another parish (and sadly missed by lots of people even after his short stay) and the first thing that happened was that my dog beat up the parish priest's dog - a gormless, hairy but affectionate old English sheepdog called Golly who also had the habit of sleeping across the threshold of the bathroom door. He was too gentle and big to kick out of the way, slept too profoundly to be woken up by a prod but inevitably shot up when one tried to step over him causing one to do the splits. He brought forth the complaint from Bishop Grant that not only did he have to consider the temperament of parish priests and curates when making appointments; he also had to keep in mind the habits and foibles of their dogs!

A resident curate was becoming a matter of some urgency, especially at week-ends, and since neither myself nor the parish priest wanted to wind down activities in Thrapston, more and more often a 'loose' priest was imported to help out. This meant that if the rather absent minded parish priest forgot to warn me I would turn up at night to find a stranger occupying my room. The crunch came when I returned after midnight on a Saturday after having run a dance or something out in the country and found a Chinaman asleep in my bed. He woke up, smiled sweetly and explained he was there for the week-end Masses. Dog and me returned to sleep in the sacristy and next day came to an amicable agreement with dog and parish priest: we would force the Bishop to send a genuine curate by the simple expedient of removing myself to Thrapston on a permanent basis - just keeping the Borstal. We went to see Bishop Grant, explained the problem, got his blessing and promise of a curate and, as an afterthought, I was given as an addition to my growing empire the town of Raunds and district which had been served from Rushden - and was declared to be a priest in charge no longer but a genuine and pukkah Parish Priest!

It did not seem to occur to anyone as to where this newly elevated parish priest was to live. The bed in the sacristy was still there but the field behind the church was bare - apart from my lodger, Tommy the donkey, who belonged to some neighbours who only had a small lawn to provide for him. It was suggested that a presbytery should be built but there was no money and I nobly claimed that I did not want to put the parish into debt; yet secretly could not bear the thought of living with architects and builders and furnishing and being responsible for a new house. I found a 28 foot ancient caravan costing £150 and hauled it, at dead of night with an unregistered tractor, on to its new site just behind the sacristy; the illegal bit being not just of academic interest. The local police station with a resident constable (fortunately an excellent Catholic) was dead opposite the church. The wheels were taken off and swapped for a load of breezeblocks and the new presbytery snugly set down on them, a foot or so off the ground. It was clad with overlapping fencing boards on the outside, lined with oak ply on the inside, had a wood burning stove, electricity and water conducted from the church and bottled gas for further heating and any culinary extravaganza that might be necessary (God had not yet given us the great gift and salvation for idiot cooks - microwave ovens). There was a small sitting room and a tiny kitchen which could be reached from the bed of the equally tiny bedroom so that the coffee could be put on first thing in the morning just by stretching out one's right arm to reach the gas cooker Except when the first frost came when the bottled gas was found to be frozen solid - easily cured by getting propane rather than the blue-bottled gas. It was all very cosy and practical and all mine! It forced one to be moderately neat and tidy but has left me with a permanent cubby-hole mentality. I spent some eight years in that caravan and had no complaints except in heavy rain when it became rather noisy and when, in spite of the solid breezeblock foundation, the needle on my record player slid and scratched the record every time my Butch jumped on or off the bed.

Raunds seemed pleased to have their very own and semi-resident priest. When under the Rushden regime they had bought a small chapel from the primitive Methodists. It was solid, central and boasted a small hall in the back. As was customary with such chapels, it was set up high with six or seven steep steps making access for the aged somewhat difficult (but possible) and the bringing in and out of a coffin quite an adventure. It would never have passed modern Health and Safety regulations. The flat ceiling was bulging down somewhat but hiding some beautiful and original gabled timber. The benches were not meant for Catholic devotions involving kneeling down and the altar was just a table. We all took some six weeks off daily religion (still kept Sundays holy and transported the locals to the Thrapston church), brought down the ceiling, painted the timbers, pulled out the benches from their wall anchorages and made new ends, spaced them out, made kneelers, painted them a less severe black but still melancholy brown, fashioned a Communion rail and sanctuary stools from beautiful Japanese oak and built an altar from the same but encompassing a very ancient carved oak panel as a centrepiece.

It was quite a transformation and great to be able to get out of the daily monkey suit which made even me look like a truly professional chippy. All my carpentry was a 'screw and glue' job and in no way true joinery but it seemed to last - until some ten or fifteen years later when it was reported that the then incumbent, being a much bigger and better man than me, suddenly caused his presidential chair (as the new liturgy insists on calling it) to collapse without warning half way through Mass. It caused some cruel hilarity in the congregation, fortunately did not harm the priest but did irreparable harm to my reputation as a carpenter.

Chapter VII continued

With Raunds came a few more villages which were searched for hidden Catholics in the now familiar manner, through village shops and pubs. There was one village pub which at lunchtime was never 'manned'. It was just open and the locals helped themselves and paid for what they drank. It seemed to work but eventually the landlord retired and the place was metamorphosed into a glass and chrome emporium with all the atmosphere, friendliness and trust gone for ever and the clientele changing at a stroke from ploughman's lunch customers to 'outsiders' arriving in convertibles, souped up Mini-Coopers and Porshes. Village shops were beginning to close, unable to cope with supermarket opposition. The locals still wanted their own shop but only for trifling things and what they may have forgotten to buy on their weekly 'big' shopping trip or the odd bit of sugar or milk which they suddenly found they were lacking and to obtain which they would not hesitate to rouse the local shopkeeper even after hours. The ultimate was a lady who went into the local post office/shop, bought nothing but asked for change to pay her bus fare to the supermarket.

With all this pub crawling - all in the very best of taste and for most noble reasons - I count myself fortunate not only not to have become an alcoholic but also not have acquired a reputation as a boozer. The danger only occurred to me much later as I thought back on cold winter evenings in the caravan when a bit of the hard stuff would probably have warmed the cockles, done little harm but possibly would have become a habit. Somehow - a blessing for which one ought to be grateful

- the temptation to drink alone has never raised its ugly head and the advice of the old rector of the seminary was quite easy to follow: "Never drink spirits regularly before the age of 40."

Meanwhile, the Diocese was split and I managed to give away four villages on the border; including Molesworth American base which had first been a military prison, then a centre for the sale of surplus stores and, by then, the home of a special force of fighter bombers with a secret compound where, it was rumoured, some unmentionable weapons were being kept. I was introduced - through a stout wire fence - to a pack of most vicious guard dogs that spent their life protecting this compound and the American military policeman who was a parishioner assured me that if he was ever called upon to do some serious work then a catastrophe of some sort would already have happened. I did not ask for further details especially when both he and I fell into disgrace with his charming Liverpudlian wife. After the tour of the base we had a drink in the mess, he had several more than was really wise and on the way back he drove over and injured a pheasant. To save it further suffering I suggested we ought to kill it in the obvious way of driving over the writhing body. The softy refused to do this and when I did the mercy killing with a large spanner he vomited spectacularly. I took the body with me to be presented to my mother for conversion into a tasty lunch. Our strong policeman eventually got home, told his story to his wife and then fell going upstairs to bed. She was genuinely shocked not just at a priest killing a pheasant but also that I could have led her innocent husband - a macho military cop - astray to such an extent that he was so inebriated as to fall up - not down - the stairs.

The world - and the Church - in the 1960/70's was going through what Heraclitus would have called a state of constant change and flux (one of those snippets of useless information sticking in the mind from two years of Philosophy). The language of the Mass was changing and Latin was no longer being taught in seminaries. Priests were moving, leaving and becoming 'specialists'. The liturgy was turned back to front; altars brought forward, communion rails torn down, the Penny Catechism not just being priced out of business but being supplanted by various catechetical schemes for children which were being acclaimed as the best since sliced bread. All this affected even the backwoods in the diocese with a parish priest dragging his feet and established parishioners - many of venerable age and a lifetime of devotion to the Church - found it all just too much. One lovely old lady sadly decided that the Mass in English just was not valid. She gently told me that she was aware that as an official representative of Holy Mother Church I was unable to resist the changes and even should not do so. But she decided that she would no longer leave her cottage in an isolated village to attend Mass - she would say it with us, in Latin, on Sundays and weekdays at the appropriate time and would be with us in spirit. I took her Holy Communion once a week and waited for the inevitable and logical consequence: she was an educated lady and would quickly reason that Communion, the Real Presence brought about by and through an 'invalid' Mass was itself suspect, to say the least. Very soon she said just that and made it clear that I would always be welcome but please don't bring her Communion. She was in her late 80's, pleading and argument only upset her further, she continued to say her own Mass and I feel certain the Lord listened to her prayers and did not hold her views against her. She died alone and - one hopes - peacefully, was not found for several days and I buried her with a Latin Mass and utter confidence in her salvation.

It was decided - I decided, since there was no such thing as even an inkling of democracy in parishes at the time - but with some consultation and advice, to run Thrapston and Raunds as one parish with as much done in common or at least on a rotation system as was possible. People were encouraged to attend the Sunday Mass at a time that suited them, no matter which end of the parish they happened to live. Easter services and Midnight Mass alternated between churches. It took a year or so for the 'them and us' mentality to be eroded - from both ends of the new parish. The histories of the areas were quite different (Raunds had been started by the now extinct Travelling Mission and always looked to

Rushden; Thrapston went back further and still tended to feel it was a part of Wellingborough or even Oundle) but since both shared a common burden - me - things gradually came together and a genuine new parish was beginning to form.

Money was always a problem. Never insuperable but many things could have been done if there had been a bit more of it. The collections gradually increased from the first Sunday grand total of just over £16 but so did expenses once the church - then churches - was used more than just on Sundays. Heating and lighting was bad enough but the great expense was transport since the only way to keep the district together was to travel a lot oneself and also bring people together. To this end we purchased an old ambulance - complete with original bell which was transferred to the sanctuary - and grandly called it the Parish Bus. The aluminium body was in excellent condition and by visiting a few scrap yards the ten-seater was converted into a comfortable fourteen seater. On three days a week it became a common sight in designated villages picking up the Catholic children straight from their school gates, taking them to one or the other church for lessons and preparations for the sacraments before distributing them more or less to their doors and hour or so later.

It demanded a certain amount of skill and dedication to drive and maintain the bus and there may well have been laws about standing passengers (certainly no rules about seat belts) but we chose to know nothing about such details. The record was a load of 30 adults being gingerly delivered back to their villages after the annual fete. It resulted in yet another visit to the scrappy to get a 'new' suspension unit. I developed a very intimate relationship with the engine (positioned inside the cab) and kept it running through the years with loving tender care - helped and supervised at every step by a good and incredibly tolerant and generous friend who owned a garage. On one occasion, quite late at night after a Bingo session, the float in the carburettor sprung a leak and we managed to get home with me driving with my right hand and very carefully pouring petrol into the open carburettor from a gallon can in my left. A spillage onto the hot exhaust may well have made that evening quite exciting. On another occasion my careless driving under a low arch resulted in the roof being neatly sliced off. Replacing it with aluminium sheets resurrected the bus but it never looked the same again and eventually had to be retired - sold for £20 to become a chicken house on a local allotment. The bell is still in the church.

We managed financially, parishioners were generous, numbers grew gradually and the parish priest got a job at £40 per month - he became Parish Clerk for Thrapston Council - mainly due to the fact that he was the only applicant who had a typewriter and duplicator. This involved attending the monthly parish meeting and issuing minutes, paying the groundsman his wages every week, allotting spaces in the local graveyard and making sure the gravedigger did his job in time and paying the quarterly bill for local street lighting. This last job nearly resulted in a coronary when the first bill arrived - well over £900! - until it became clear it was for the Thrapston Parish, not St. Paul's Catholic Parish. On odd occasions it did appear rather unfair that bigger and more established neighbouring parishes could afford to spend more money on various luxuries - new liturgical accoutrements apparently being 'demanded' by the new liturgy, fancy books, kneelers, pilfer-proof collection baskets etc etc - than we ever had to spend on necessities. On one occasion (a quite convivial clerical Christmas party) one parish priest matter-of-factly mentioned that he had spent as much on a new duvet as we managed to get in a whole month's income. And there was me with my faithful companion - Butch - acting as an excellent hot water bottle. In years to come I did remember this incident and when in bigger and richer parishes did consider it a lawful parish expense to help smaller or newer parishes by offering to pay some of their less huge bills - if only as a sign of good will.

My mother moved into a small bungalow in Raunds, well knowing the risk that a move for me would eventually be on the cards. To her eternal credit she never interfered in the parish and was quite happy not to have any preferential treatment. I did often wonder how strange it must have been for her to listen week after week to her son's brilliant sermons but never actually dared to ask just in case she would be brutally honest. Who knows, she may well have just switched off! Parishioners were very good to her, she made many friends and seemed to be happy. I remained in the caravan but more often than not travelled the five miles to have a good lunch rather than 'enjoy' my own brand of cooking - microwaves, the saviours of old and crusty bachelors, were only just being invented. The Borstal had become a thing of the past and my apparently indispensable job in the Corby schools had been taken over by a resident priest. There was more than enough to do in that scattered parish - not to mention my growing notoriety as an odd ball who gave shelter to Thomas the donkey, slept with his dog, had all kinds of contacts for getting puppies and kittens for old people who had lost their pets, had a thriving non-profit making organisation with the local S.V.P. chopping up liberally grease-soaked barrels used for bringing in sheep fleeces from Australia to the local tanneries and so distributing bundles of kindling to old people in remote corners of Northamptonshire and, even, having the biggest pipe collection in the area. With no real ambition to speak of I would probably have been more than happy if I had stayed in the place for good. Whether the same could be said for the parishioners was not something I really wanted to know since in rare introspective moments I did begin to think that perhaps we were all getting into a rut, except for the nagging sense of guilt that a house really ought to be built to give the place some respectability. When, after ten years, the move to Bedford came, the lack of a house made it very difficult for the poor bishop to find a priest to take over. It was a comfortable, scruffy and cosy way to live; with a few obvious limitations, but certainly not to everyone's taste. Bishop Grant phoned one day and asked, would I like to go to Bedford. My reply was: "Not really". He then characteristically made it impossible to argue by saying that *it would make him very happy if I went to Bedford. Who was I to refuse to make a bishop happy? So I went.*

Even just two weeks before the change was due there was no replacement for the parish and I was on the verge of rebellion; it seemed like treachery to leave the place priestless. At the bishop's request several likely candidates had been along, admired the churches, loved the landscape, expressed wonder at the parish bus and some concern about the level of income (I had been on the list of 'poor parishes' organised by the Universe Catholic paper whereby at Christmas and Easter a large and generous food parcel was delivered to keep the parish priest alive and kicking for the big feasts) but expressed horror at living in a caravan - even though there was a definite Episcopal promise that a house could be built at any time. Presumably the general lot of curates had improved since they turned down the offer of a parish - never mind the idea of obedience - when just a few years previously no self-respecting and suffering curate would have refused the offer of even a cabbage patch. Eventually a lovely priest was appointed who proved utterly unable to look after himself - never mind the material side of a parish - in any practical way and nearly starved through the next twelve months or so. It was cruel and very unfair on an excellent priest with much to offer but as unable to be practical as I am of being artistic or becoming a violin virtuoso. Both he and the parish survived, he went on to give valuable service in other parishes, Thrapston and Raunds and scattered district went through some pains and changes but emerged still a parish and now, no doubt, ready to be 'clustered' or undergo whatever the future may hold for most areas.

I was given a generous cheque by the parishioners (a touching and life-saving custom which could also mean that it assures one's departure and little likelihood of coming back) plus a very posh and engraved pipe lighter/cleaner and departed to a much larger parish in Bedford - still with quite a few villages attached so that my pub-crawling with a pious purpose could continue. It was only some 18 miles away from where my mother had settled down so keeping my eye on her - and vice versa - was still quite easy and whether Bishop Grant had had this in mind or not, she remained convinced that he had been deliberately helpful and understanding and she always had a soft spot for him; not to mention that on visitations and confirmations he had always had a good meal and short nap at her bungalow and made a fuss of her cat. A contrast to his brief incursions into the caravan where he had been obliged to remain permanently stooped.

Reflection

*Our Lady of Walsingham

I turn to every man and woman, including those who have fallen away from the Church, who have left the faith or who have never heard the proclamation of salvation.

To everyone the Lord says, "Behold, I stand at the door and knocked: if anyone hears my voice and opens the door, I will come to him and eat with him, and he with me [Rev 3.290]*

For the animals of God's creation

* this to go with the Donley and Pigs Each creature has its own being; at the same time it is related not only to other beings but to God

All Beings pay you homage, those that think and those that cannot.

The universal desire, the profaning of all creation , aspires towards you. Towards you all beings that can read your Universe raise a hymn of silence. The movement of the Universe surges towards you. Of all beings you are the goal, you who are beyond all things.

St Gregory of Nazianzen [c.330-89]

Chapter VIII

Bedford

The priest in Bedford had been in the parish some four years and had made a great impression on it. He was gifted, energetic, modern and charismatic, especially in the Liturgy, which enabled him to do naturally all kinds of things that I found to be embarrassing if not impossible. The house was a three bedroom semi right opposite the church and perfectly adequate as a presbytery but huge in comparison to what I had been used to and with stairs which even Butch treated with some suspicion to begin with. There was an 'open house' policy so that all and sundry had free access at any time. There was also the mystery of the locked bedroom. Apparently there was a 'lodger' - something which had not been mentioned and filled me, a hermit, with some foreboding. On my third night there, very late, Butch went mad on hearing someone coming into the house and proceeding upstairs into the said locked room. It was the lodger; a young man who was thinking of, perhaps, going on to the priesthood. We had an amicable discussion and agreed that his stay would be limited - he seemed as keen to go as I was to see him go, if only because he was terrified of dogs; never mind a new and strange parish priests. The confrontation was friendly and I would like to think it did not affect the fact that the lad never did go on to a seminary. Quite quickly the free and random access, and the weekday nursery school downstairs from 9.00 till 4.00 - were curtailed, although meetings etc were, of course, continued. Surprisingly many individuals made me feel less guilty about this by saying that an open house had quite often made it difficult to see a priest in confidence and they never knew who would open the door or how active the place might be. The domestic changes did not seem to cause much distress or upheaval in the parish. One gentleman did point out quite strongly that the house was not mine; it belonged to the parish. We agreed on that legal aspect of it but decided to disagree on how that should be interpreted in practice and we have remained on good terms since.

The church was a modern one, quite big, square and with a floor sloping down towards the sanctuary. It took a while to get used to walking downhill towards the altar but was, presumably, what architects are wont to call 'a feature' [even though on one occasion a little boy kept on rolling his orange down the hill to my feet while I was preaching and - not perhaps wisely - I kept on throwing it back to him]. Perhaps it did even facilitate the view of the altar and priest for the usual crowd of Catholics who always sit at the back, Yet one more mystery of my religion. It is a modern, functional church, but had little of the traditional aura of a place of worship - changed through the years now by the addition of a few statues, beautiful altar and some stained glass windows. As a loyal and obedient priest and a natural extrovert as well, my predecessor had introduced many aspects of the new liturgy, had several flourishing music groups with guitars and percussion instruments, enjoyed the services of two or three good organists, keen singers, servers and general organisers who all made it easy for this country bumpkin to merge in and not disrupt things or try to mend them if they ain't bust.

The Sunday Sign of Peace - going down the aisle and actually kissing Catholics - was beyond me, I explained, and it was cheerfully accepted. The 'Movers' - consisting of nubile young ladies in leotards dancing towards the altar at the Offertory (thankfully only performed once a month) and then holding hands with the priest - was an artistic and perfectly proper interpretation of lay participation in the Mass. But it was a surprise, not to say shock, which left me so obviously speechless and ill at ease that, after two or three months the ceremony was quietly dropped without anyone having to take any draconian measures. It would be nice to think that the change-over did not have too traumatic an effect on the parish and certainly no changes were consciously brought in just for the sake of change.

I missed my own lodger - Tommy the donkey - but still had the dog and free access to a whole zoo of sometimes exotic animals housed at the Convent some two miles away. The Sisters were charming and helpful in all ways, Sunday Masses there were a joy (even though the church was circular and when preaching one could not help wondering what the congregation behind one's back might be getting up to), the grounds vast and there was a standing invitation and welcome to share lunch with the Sisters and any various visitors or attendees at retreats, study sessions etc who might be there. I was aware of the temptation to rely too much on the good will of the Sisters and abuse their willingness to help - whether in the Liturgy or instructions or even domestic chores - and suspect I did keep what might, at times, have appeared as a snooty aloofness. The knowledge that there was always that background and support, plus having an eager and able parishioner who dealt with all financial matters made the change to a big parish much easier than I had feared and expected.

I hardly slept for the first few nights. Not because of the heavy burden of cares for a new and much bigger parish but because of the traffic. Used to living in a field with no neighbours and a street some 100 yards away and hearing only Tommy's heavy breathing as he huddled for shelter against the caravan wall it was rather disconcerting to have late night revellers belting past, changing gears to negotiate the roundabout only to accelerate away again - often with ICE (for the uninitiated: In-car- entertainment) going at full blast. But priests are as adaptable as the rest of mankind and I soon got used to urban noises; even to people banging on the door much more regularly, frequently and at all kinds of hours than I ever experienced in the wilds of Northamptonshire.

One early morning - about 2.00 a.m. when for some reason I was still up, typing and listening to music - the doorbell rang and, as a wise precaution, I took my Butch with me to open the front door. The streetlight just outside was out (Bedford Town Council used to save public money by extinguishing some lights at midnight) and in the meagre illumination from the porch I saw a figure in a white suit - and no head! - standing on the doorstep. It only seemed so for a second but the hairs on the back of my neck stood to attention and Butch growled ominously - until the man spoke and it became obvious that it was the figure of a very black man dressed to kill. He was charming, had spent the evening in his best suit with his girlfriend and had a terrible row with her. He was very upset, had a coffee, liked the dog, calmed down and went off home with what I hoped was good advice - to go back next day with due penitence and red roses. I did not know him from Adam and never heard from him again.

Another late night saw a young lady being abandoned on the doorstep by a 'friend' and claiming she was possessed by the devil. She looked a bit dishevelled and distressed but we discussed the matter, telephoned her mother somewhere in Oxfordshire and went into the church at dead of night since the girl claimed her devil would not allow her to enter churches. He/she/they did not seem to mind, we talked a bit more about the whole subject, said a prayer and by the time the mother arrived the devil seemed to have gone - not surprisingly, perhaps; the mother turned out to be a formidable lady - and my nocturnal visitor was calm and demure and asked to receive Holy Communion. Rightly or wrongly, liturgically and spiritually correct or not, she did receive Communion there and then very devoutly, went off with Mum and - as so often happens - I never heard from either of them - or that particular devil - again.

Bedford being synonymous with John Bunyan there were some celebrations just about to start marking the tercentenary of - I think - the publication/writing of Pilgrim's Progress, since it was the turn of a Catholic priest to be the chairman of the local ecumenical gathering the other Catholic priests in Bedford all ganged up and gave me the job for the year. Not only did I not know any of the civic or ecclesiastical worthies but I also found - and still do find - Ecumenism in action quite difficult. Without any qualifications whatever I respect the views of others and their right to keep to them. I even envy so many things other Christians have which are not quite so obvious in our Church - the singing skill and prowess of Methodists, the knowledge of and familiarity with the Bible, the much more personal relationship with Jesus (rather than the more distant form of address of 'Our Lord'), the organisation and genuine lay participation in parishes; to mention just a few. But I find that actually indulging in what I affectionately but possibly flippantly call 'mixed bathing' is full of pitfalls, hidden landmines, traps and possibilities of quite innocently causing offence and even hurt. So I blundered through the year with lots of meetings, a few processions, risking my life guarding the Bishop of St. Albans from being crushed as he preached by the statue of John Bunyan bang in the centre of town with lorries mounting the pavement as they negotiated the tight left turn on their way to Goldington and Cambridge, playing host to T.V. celebrities and even - most horrible of all - having a breakfast meeting (!) of clergy at 7.00 a.m. in the presbytery. It was a relief to end my year of duty without having started a war of religion and - as far as I know - doing the ecumenical movement irreparable harm.

More relaxed but still an experience I would rather not repeat was the customary Corpus Christi procession organised - using the term loosely - from the main old church in the town centre and which the 'new boy' in town was press-ganged to lead. It was the proud boast of the old Monsignor there that Bedford was home to 44 nationalities and he tried to involve as many of these as possible in the procession each year. They gathered, dressed in national costumes, and were encouraged to sing a verse or two of their favourite hymn in their own language. All this caused severe congestion in the town centre around the church and delayed the start of the procession by a good hour.

Eventually some semblance of order was restored and I carried the Monstrance, watched with bemused interest by the local inhabitants, followed by a good congregation and preceded by an assortment of servers. Those carrying 'torches' used them, off and on, to have mock sword fights, the singing of hymns - as always in processions - varied by a musical bar or so from the front to the back of the straggly line. The highlight, however, which I found strangely moving, was when we reached a crossroads and the policeman on duty - a Sergeant - having stopped all the traffic, then stood rigidly to attention and saluted the passing of the Real Presence. It was a simple but very public act of faith and respect in contrast to the utter lack of interest shown by practically all the bystanders, passers-by and other people milling around pursuing whatever might have been their business.

As it happened, this was the last such public procession. Future ones took place in school grounds or out in the beautiful environment of Clapham Convent. It is debatable whether it is better to do this and avoid the 'scoffing of the multitude' (even just complete indifference) or to show one's faith publicly even if the public as a whole has no idea what is going on.

There were Catholic schools in Bedford and my quite false reputation as some sort of expert had preceded me so that in no time at all, with no really valid excuses to offer, I was a Governor, a correspondent, a chaplain and general factotum in all of them. Changes in the age structure were just being introduced and plans were near fruition for an Upper School to be built on my doorstep. Bishop Grant dug the first sod - with some difficulty since we had just had a long period of good weather and the soil was rock hard - and there was a lot of involvement in the building, planning, appointment of Head and teachers, governors and, of course, raising money to pay for it all.

Although the parish was a big one and there was more than enough work, the abiding memory is of being swamped by school business. It may well be that - if remembered at all - my ten years there were only remarkable for my dog(s), the vision of a little fellow belting around on a big motorbike and the quaint manner of heating the church - which was big, square, high and had electric under-floor heating. This was yet another architectural 'feature' and consisted of the floor area being divided into three sections which, when heated, did do the job very well, even though the cost was rather high. However, on my arrival one third of the area had already ceased to function and within a few weeks the second third also became defunct. Incredible though it may seem, to repair the wiring the whole section of floor, tiles and cement - would have had to be lifted and re-laid at great expense and inconvenience. My plebeian solution was to wheel in two monstrous paraffin blowers or, a more genteel description, 'space heaters'. They did the job but were ugly, horrendously noisy, had an insatiable appetite for fuel and generally reminded people of a couple of jet engines on the loose. They had to be switched off for Mass and their effect reproduced, as far as possible, by hot air from the pulpit!

By the end of my undistinguished career in Bedford I was Chairman of Governors of five schools, chaplain to two of them and on the Bedfordshire County Council Education Committee - all part-time jobs over and above normal parish work. All this while my faith in the value of Catholic schools in general was gradually being eroded at more or less the same time that politicians were starting to interfere with education as a whole and changes in structure seemed almost to be a daily event.

It is difficult to make any criticism of Catholic Education because the whole subject has been a 'sacred cow' and remains as such. It is also a personal opinion which is not shared by everyone by any means. We have spent untold money and effort on our schools through the years to the detriment of our parishes. Most of our schools by far are academically excellent and the staff fully trained, committed and beyond reproach. They have what many call a 'Catholic ethos' which does set them apart from other schools. But they do not seem to be able to 'form' young people to practice their faith and certainly do not produce informed, committed, and practising Catholics. They encourage all this and churn out the right information, even have lots of pupils passing public and diocesan religious exams but fall into what I consider to be the general trap when it comes to religious education, formation and upbringing.

If you would rather not be scandalised then don't read on!

Through the years I have heard innumerable people say that when they were children they were made to go to church, Sunday school, lessons etc and were put off 'religion' because of it. We also insist on treating children as special, different, 'the church of the future', to be spoon-fed with watered down services specially adapted for guitars and pop music, to be told things like " Christmas is a children's feast" etc.

That is the trap. Children and young people tend to grow up and grow out of and pass on from this youthful and immature period and, having matured in all other things, find ......nothing; they have not been allowed to mature in the practice of their relationship with God - their religion. They have been isolated from their families, their community, the adults they so soon become.

They are taught to read and write, to have good manners, to use a knife and fork, to support Arsenal (or not), to respect their elders and their neighbours, to pay their bus fares and be kind to animals, all this in the environment in which they live with their family. They are not given lessons in such things divorced from their family, in a kind of vacuum or just from 9.00 to 4.00 in term time. If, if it should happen that they do not have this background, their family uses their fingers to eat and terrorises the old lady next door then teaching them to do something else is an uphill struggle and will seldom take root. If even at school they are surrounded by young people whose family is thus lacking, then that becomes the norm and even takes the form of 'peer pressure', no matter what may be on the syllabus or what the 'ethos' may be.

Yet that is what we do with our schools. Especially the upper, senior or secondary schools; let's say from 11 upwards. As small children in junior schools there is every opportunity to teach and practise the basics of our relation with God and neighbour and parents are far more willing and able to supplement this and, for the sake of the child, teach by example. Thus we ought to leave our junior schools to continue the excellent work they are doing --- BUT make it clear that children will not automatically go up to senior schools just because they have attended the feeder school and been baptised. They must be or must become or be in the process of becoming genuine, practising, Mass going Catholics - within their family and with their brothers and sisters. Our upper schools should be prepared to close down unless they are filled with pupils who are such active Catholics or, at the very least, are making genuine efforts to be part of the worshipping (not just baptised) Catholic community.

This is real revolutionary doctrine. Some may say it is extreme and fanatical and, put into effect, could well close our senior schools, in which case we ought to be able to use the saving in effort and money on parish or community support - not for youth or children but for the family as a whole. It should be made clear that unless the family as a whole is involved in the practice of their religion then their child cannot attend a Catholic school. It may well be simplistic and brutal; bleeding hearts will complain bitterly that we cannot force people to become Mass goers; we must not blackmail them into worshipping God.

It is not at all what is proposed.

What is being asked is: "Why do you want your child to attend a Catholic school? Is it fair to him/her to be taught one thing at school and another at home? Is it fair, even at a financial level, that the 10% of parents and children who actively support our parishes and pay for the schools should subsidise the other 90%? And even more fundamentally, should the ethos and practice and general atmosphere and 'peer pressure' of that purely nominally Catholic 90% affect and make it difficult for the 10% and the whole purpose of our Catholic schools?"

Going back 20 years or more and recalling and now meeting again young people who had gone through the whole Catholic school system it is incredible how shallow is their knowledge of their faith and how very few ever go to church, get married there, have their children baptised. Little things that you would think would stick in their minds for ever (unimportant, perhaps, but pegs on which a relationship with God could be hung - how many sacraments are there? Do you know the 'Hail Mary'? Who are the four Evangelists? Why go to Mass? Is dodging your bus fare wrong? Why pray for dead people? Is contraception O.K.? etc etc etc) are simply not known; met with a blank look as if one were asking about the intimate religious practices of the Aztecs - yet they remember and practise the rules of soccer, value their examination results and have gone on to further studies in their chosen subjects and have matured in all other ways.

What is really tragic is that so many parents have been sending their children to Catholic senior schools, supported those schools in every way, practised their religion, have been active members of parishes and found that their children got so immersed in and overwhelmed by the general pupil attitude in those schools that their own teaching and example - even pleading - has had no effect whatever. They have been saddened and shocked by their children saying: "Nobody believes it. None of the kids go to church. They all do it (whatever it may be). Get a life, Mum/Dad." And they ask themselves - and priests - "Where have we as parents gone wrong?"

Change cannot be brought about by any one school, it cannot be done unilaterally and in isolation by all our upper schools together. The fostering and growth of faith and the practice of it does have to be based on knowledge and information but is not assured by passing examinations, a tiny minority of pupils going off on a retreat or doing a religious musical, supporting good causes, no matter how worthy or religious they may be, having voluntary school Masses on a Tuesday afternoon, no matter how well they may be attended.

Of course all these things do help; as do all kinds of excellent initiatives promoted by the Diocese, parishes, school staff and anxious and generous parents. But it has to be supported by the parish, the community, the form of worship and liturgy, the involvement of each whole family and specifically a very blunt and authoritative and often repeated statement - supported by an official admissions policy - that parents cannot shuffle off their responsibility by sending their children to a Catholic school and expect that school to make them Catholics.

If even some of these things were to be done - and urgently - then the senior Catholic schools that survive would be a support to and extension of the Catholic families and community. They could afford to integrate a very limited number of non-Catholic pupils (never, say over 15%, and in order to offer our cherished ethos to others - not seek to convert them - and to avoid making our schools water-tight units in the community as a whole). Most schools would close because of spectacularly reduced numbers. The funds and human skills and good will could then be used on a parish or district level to provide religious knowledge and continue to support faith and practice - not in crèches, youth clubs, exclusively youth-based jolly and fashionable liturgies (and how long do fashions or fads or being 'with it' last?) new ' best since the invention of sliced bread' catechetical courses - but in practical and simple courses for the families as they grow and struggle to maintain their relationship with God through the Church.

This 'verging on the violent' attitude to our senior schools has developed gradually. For many years I had doubts and fears about it all but hoped for the best, presumed things would change for the better and the situation had not been aggravated by 'falling numbers', 'catchments areas', 'surplus places' and other mantras suffered every month in the Education Committee and by our concentrated effort to fill our schools, have bums on seats, even if the percentage of non-Catholic pupils grew year by year. Milton Keynes was still lacking an upper school and to provide education at secondary level to the children there as well as fill our own school with Catholic pupils we spent a lot of time and raised a fortune to run our own transport to and from M.K. I even practised driving a 35 seat coach and often acted as shotgun on various busses in a usually vain attempt to calm down the more unruly passengers. By a tortuous and Jesuitical form of argument in the Committee I even managed to slip 60 plus 'imported' pupils over and above the number the County had allowed for and reckoned with. Several members commented that I was wasted in the Church and ought to become a politician - I still have doubts whether this was meant as a compliment.

The parish ran smoothly - I think - with lots of parishioner involvement, as few changes as possible while still remaining inside the diocesan/liturgical laws and all the experimentations taking place through those years, the usual First Communions and Confirmations and a constant and running battle to be able to use school halls for parish social functions without having to pay exorbitant hiring fees. We even once used the church (moving all the hefty benches) for a dance but I was assured that the sloping floor made dancing uphill and/or downhill quite a challenge and the slow and smoochy waltz at the end was not quite the same in a holy and brightly lit ambience. We obtained a large statue of Our Lady in some need of decoration. It had been abandoned in the nether regions of Bishop's House and loaded on to my trailer - all six foot of her. The wind plus possibly my rate of driving tore the covers off the statue and exposed it to the wonder of all heading south on the M1. She was duly and artistically renovated and we had a Lady Altar/Chapel. House Masses were a custom which I had inherited and these continued more or less at one a week at different venues with the villages especially benefiting. In the town itself, however, the same 'usual suspects' tended to attend the same house Masses. An annual Harvest Mass was said way out in a village hall which was always beautifully decorated, really well attended and used a few bales of straw as an altar. My presence of mind one year was greatly admired: at the Consecration a wee mouse pocked his or her head out of the straw right in front of me. It was seen by one or two but I did not bat an eyelid nor pause nor hesitate and managed not to say to the ladies present: "Oh! look! A mouse!"

The silver jubilee of one's ordination is certainly a landmark but by temperament - not humble and self effacing but more like curmudgeonous - I would have preferred to celebrate it, with some surprise at lasting that long, quite privately. However, the parish made it into a big event so that it would have been incredibly churlish to reject the universal kindness shown to me. My mother attended the special 'musical extravaganza' Mass and was rewarded with a front seat and a huge bouquet of flowers rather than blame for being responsible for my existence. The bishop said nice things about me (reminiscent of priests' funerals where there is one priest lying in the pulpit and the other lying in the coffin), some 30 priests came to give moral support, the ladies prepared and served a delicious and lavish feast to all comers, the parish presented me with a cheque which made my bank manager very happy and the children decorated the church with their versions of what they thought of me. This turned out to be the only disappointment since they had put a lot of effort into their pictures, it was fascinating to see oneself as they apparently saw me but, because the wedding couple next day would not tolerate the display, all these masterpieces had to be taken down that evening. I spent the day just trying to look benevolent and not showing how touched and grateful I really was. People's acceptance of their priests and their almost universal kindness and tolerance never ceases to surprise me.

Ten or twelve years in a parish seems an ideal stretch for both priest and people. By then most of the damage will have been done and all settle down into a comfortable rut with things running predictably and smoothly and the temptation is great not to initiate too many new ideas for fear of rocking the boat. Human nature being what it is, there must be some people who cannot stand their priest, his appearance, his mannerisms, the inevitable idiosyncrasies each priest has in the way he says Mass, cracks his corny jokes. Yet they are landed with him week after week and must, by that time, be longing for a change. It is easier for a priest since he relates to many people and the congregation does change gradually as time goes on. Some priests ask to move more frequently. Others are quite happy to be left in peace and only budge when they get prodded by their bishop. After ten years in Bedford I was quite happy to remain there but had a gut feeling that changes were afoot; so kept my head down and pretended I was not there. A move is always traumatic - much more for the people of God than even for the priest.

Chapter IX

Woburn Sands

Elevated to the Council of Canons

By 1985 Fr. Edmund (Ted) Golston had been parish priest at St. Mary's Woburn Sands for 46 years! It remains one of the mysteries of our religion how this could ever have happened. He went there as a young priest just four years after I was born and certainly it would have been cruel to have moved him after the first 25 or 30 years. He was happy, his parishioners were happy and somehow (one theory is that he 'had something' on a succession of Bishops) he became an institution. For ten years or so his health had not been good and the time had come for him to feel that he should retire. At the celebration of his Golden Jubilee various priests concelebrating the Mass in the beautiful church and being feasted in the extensive grounds were casting envious eyes on the parish and, if clergy had been prone to gambling, a book would have been started as to who would inherit this 'plum' of a parish.

I did!

Through Providence, pure good luck, warped sense of humour by the Bishop (Bishop Francis Thomas by then) or for whatever reason a complete outsider who had never been considered a runner nor himself even thought of going there was made an offer he could not refuse. The Bishop said that in exchange for keeping on the schools and Education Committee would I like to go to Woburn Sands? Reminding him that, technically, I did not owe him any obedience because of the error made at my ordination, I nevertheless followed the pious practice of not arguing with bishops. The takeover date was set, by amicable negotiation, for the middle of October and since all the other moves (one move in the Diocese having the domino effect of creating six or seven others) all took place some six weeks earlier, I became officially homeless - the Bedford presbytery and parish got its new incumbent while Fr. Golston was more than welcome to take his time, wind down, make his farewells to his many friends and gradually move into retirement to Ipswich, the place of his birth.

By yet another stroke of incredible luck the Provincial House in Clapham was closing down just at this time and the Sisters were 'down-grading' to a much smaller property in Northampton. The retreat centre with its 40 or so rooms and facilities was empty, furniture and effects were being auctioned and there was every reason to suspect that any self-respecting burglar would have his greedy eyes on the place. What better protection than having a chunky priest and his Boxer dog (Butch had, sadly, gone to his reward and Bonzo taken his place) living in the centre - out of suitcases - as a night watchman in return for a comfortable bed and generous board. On several occasions young Bonzo went mad in the middle of the night and barked up and down the corridors but it is a moot point whether this was because of rabbits, wild deer or just sheer exuberance or whether he was actually putting the frighteners on prowlers and potential burglars. Nothing untoward happened, I led a peripatetic existence for several weeks going over to Woburn Sands a few times to be shown the ropes and great kindness by Fr. Golston, fed by his housekeeper sister and doing my very best not to give him the impression that he was dragging his feet a bit with the move. Hopefully I succeeded. He was a gentle and kind old gentleman and the parish had been his whole life for so long that he deserved to be given time to leave.

Eventually I moved in and all the gloomy prophecies of my fellow clergy came to be fulfilled. They all said that following a dearly loved and greatly respected priest after 40 odd years would be horrendous. Some had the theory - actually aired in front of the Bishop - that the worst, most ratty and difficult priest ought to be sent there, create havoc for six months or so and then moved out to be replaced by the real, new parish priest. People would be so glad to be rid of the awkward one that the new man would be welcomed with open arms. The Bishop smiled and indicated that, perhaps, that was exactly what he was doing! Is our custom of not consulting with parishioners (and not all that much with the priest) an advantage when new appointments are made? It is certainly simpler and quicker since few parishioners know anything of their new priest and the priest himself can always claim, when he faces disaster, that he did not ask to be moved and was just acting out of holy obedience.

Bonzo and self-stood there on a Thursday afternoon in a more or less empty house having just witnessed a large rat taking refuge from us by scampering under the old wooden hall. The house was large, the church traditional (no sloping floors, no space heaters), the grounds vast when a tall gentleman knocked on the door, regarded us sadly and stated the obvious: "You will have a job living up to Fr. Golston". It was a welcome and it was well meant but it was echoed on Sunday when people came into church and you could see them thinking exactly the same. They missed their priest and friend and many were hoping that I would become a sort of junior version.

Many - especially the older parishioners - went out of their way to welcome me, even if in a rather guarded fashion. My response was not calculated; just seemed a good idea at the time. I went round for the first three months or so being more gormless than usual, trying not to change anything deliberately, making it clear that there would be times when I would have to be doing other things than just being there, being more of a loner than ever.

Hard, manual work is a great refuge and on coming to a new parish there are always things which 'had always been so' but really did need mending because they were broke but all had got accustomed to the parish just ticking over nicely and nobody rocking the boat. The church doors of fine timber were bone dry and got several coats of linseed oil - which also meant that I was there, doing it, being seen and meeting people as they passed or dropped in to say a prayer and tell me I was putting it on upside down. When it rained the car park became a lake since the soak-away drain could not cope and "It's been like that for years, Father."

Donning my monkey suit I lowered myself some four feet into the drain to find a thick bed of gravel, papers, cigarette ends and years of debris blocking the outlet. Slowly sinking deeper as I shovelled all this out I was beginning to win, my head was still just showing over the top when the heavens opened and the whole drain was filled up again while I stood in the church porch, soaked, having a smoke and determined to finish the job now that I could not get wetter or dirtier. The rain stopped, the silt was all cleaned out and lo and behold - when it rained again the drain coped. My reputation as a drain cleaner had been established, I had a professional set of rods and no future blockages in house, church or hall ever defeated me.

In spite of every effort, things were bound to be changing and there was an unhappy feeling in the parish that this new man was not a patch on old Fr. Ted. I was out on school business one or two days a week and lots of evenings were spent at long-winded, boring and utterly useless meetings of various Governors; with the additional work caused by a new upper school about to be started in Milton Keynes. Sunday Masses had to be shifted a bit and accelerated because, now that this fit and super-efficient priest was in residence, Cranfield was returned to the parish. There was an unease, a sense of resistance, a fear that the work of 40 years would, somehow, be destroyed and lost. Christmas came round and with it the chief source of income for priests who, many do not realise, get no salary - the customary Christmas Offering. An envelope appeared containing two bright new pennies and a note - anonymous - saying: *'This might become more when you become a proper priest'.* It did nothing to make it a happier Christmas but, publishing a photocopy in the next news sheet, resulted in a miraculous change of attitude and a wave of sympathy and empathy for this odd-ball who had been inflicted on the parish.

Woburn Sands Vietnamese pot-bellied pigs

Things improved by leaps and bounds. The impossible was never achieved - pleasing everybody all the time - but the parish council was allowed to wither away to be replaced by general consultation with all, the church made more cosy with a carpet and a curtain behind the altar (the crucifix retained by popular demand even though the incumbent continued to find it 'odd'), St. Joseph lifted up so communicants going back to their places did not smash their heads on his plinth, the leaking Lady Chapel roof eventually and permanently sealed and some efforts made to discourage a certain amount of traditional isolationism by making links with neighbouring parishes.

The grounds around the house had been a vegetable and flower garden but had recently gone a bit wild and boasted one heap of healthy manure and another one of logs for the fire. Not being a gardener nor wanting the labour of an open fire a few trips with the trailer to the local tip solved that problem and a pony followed by Buster the donkey were installed to keep the grass down. Buster was six months old and a great pet, a focus of interest for parishioners young and old and featured in several newspapers and magazines - with pictures of priest and donkey being differentiated by the number of legs. More pets came along as the years went by; not all of them there all the time at the same time; Milton the sheep - who, as all sheep, started as a cuddly lamb and grew up to be huge, free range with a bell round his neck and once gate crashed a wedding ceremony; several goats who ate everything except what they were meant to eat, some pot-bellied pigs who were so ugly they were beautiful, guinea fowls who eventually flew away, two geese who disgraced themselves by nesting on a headstone in the cemetery and had to be deported, ducks, chickens, turkeys for Christmas (but the fox got them during Advent), noisy cockerels who caused neighbours to complain, were too fast to catch in daylight and roosted up a tree at night (had to shoot them down with a double-barrelled shotgun - legally acquired and held!); barn owls and kestrels plus some chipmunks who were incredibly swift and eventually made their escape to live wild for a few months and, of course, dogs and a lovely cat called Smokey.

The donkey of St Mary's

Clapham Convent had closed and the chapel was in the process of being dismantled. The altar and tabernacle went to a church in Bedford while the mosaic of Our Lady stood outside, forlorn, unwanted and going begging. Off I went with my trusty trailer, nobody having told me just how incredibly heavy this mosaic really was, levered it on and set off only to have the undercarriage collapse at the Clapham Road roundabout. There was no way it could be abandoned there, no AA man would accept it as a natural breakdown, so I hauled it - wheel-less - all the way to St. Thomas More school car park; leaving a double scar in the tarmac marking my passage. Next day a builder friend and strong assistant loaded it on a lorry and brought it to Woburn Sands where it can now be seen displayed in all its splendour. A parishioner designed and erected the shrine and the whole undertaking met with universal approval - almost.

One lady complained bitterly and repeatedly that she could not now see her mother's grave as she approached the cemetery until she actually reached the gates. You can't win 'em all!

The rat that had scuttled off on my first arrival lived comfortably with his extended family under the old wooden hall which had served the parish well through the years but was certainly now on its last legs. Discussions about a new hall got bogged down on the prohibitive cost for a even a humble one. Through a stalwart parishioner a local builder came forward and offered to build a new hall to the tune of Â£ 100,000 - free - on the one condition: that we name it after his mother-in-law who had died recently. My instant response was that we would gladly call it 'Beelzebub's Den' if required, we shook hands on the deal, the news was announced, plans displayed and work started more or less immediately. Most people were overjoyed and amazed but surprisingly many found the whole thing a threat complaining that a new building would cut down the grass area, would change the nature of the parish, would shatter the peace of the place, would create a security risk and be a magnet for vandals and why not build it on the same side as the house and - one lady insisted - the entrance should face the cemetery, not the car park.

It occurred to me that the Diocese ought to be told about this deal and how it would enhance the value of the parish. The financial gurus went berserk. No contract had been signed, the builder would charge us a fortune, no matter what his offer or promise may have been, ownership would be disputed, the scheme had not been considered nor approved by Diocesan architects, surveyors and planners and no estimates had been invited on a competitive basis. By heroic and suicidal efforts I managed to keep Diocese and Builder from actually meeting face to face since threats on the telephone nearly resulted in the whole offer being withdrawn. Finally the Bishop 'happened' to drop in, looked at the foundations being laid, confirmed that the whole thing was a bit unorthodox but since I was the person in charge of the parish he would leave the whole matter to me and trust in my judgement. Quite touched and greatly relieved, the work progressed, the hall was built, the area of car park doubled, the exit on to the main road made less of a Russian roulette and - eventually - even the doubters had to accept that it was a great asset and a promise faithfully fulfilled to the tune of £120,000; of which the parish paid some £8,000 through the years as a sign of good will while the rest was finally written off the builder's books and the hall is all ours with no strings attached - and myself avoiding unfrocking by a whisker.

Am not sure what happened to the rat(s).

The years went by with all the usual parish activities, spiritual and social, the local population increasing, a real chapel being acquired at Cranfield through the good offices of the natives and the generosity of the University authorities, the cemetery was quietly extended by letting the old fence fall and erecting a new one a bit further down our field (on the old principle that if you don't ask for permission to extend then you won't get a refusal), the church was internally decorated without recourse to the Liturgy Commission nor Architect (it was white and blue and remained the same so nobody other than the locals noticed) and after ten years or more I was not seeking to move but willing to practise some more obedience if required but otherwise keeping my head down. New laws made it illegal for anyone to be a Governor of more than two schools at the same time. Which let me off the hook a bit and gradually, encouraged by my growing lack of conviction in the whole principle of Catholic schools, I managed to palm off all my jobs. The County Education Council was re-formed and this gave me the perfect opportunity to resign with due dignity and lose the only perks the job ever had - free parking under County Hall and access at any time to make a cup of coffee and have a free biscuit.

To make life interesting and avoid any danger of getting into the proverbial rut, I broke my leg and had lengthy complications resulting in many months of living on pain killers, saying Mass sitting on a bar stool behind the altar and ruining many a wedding photograph by perching on crutches between bride and groom. For the first week I drove my own car using my right leg to depress the clutch. It was pointed out that this was an illegal and lethal practice and my insurance company would not be happy. A generous parishioner let me use a large automatic Mercedes for about eight weeks which made me feel like a bishop until it came to filling up the tank and I found that it did about 15 miles a gallon. After a bit the gear changes on my own car became possible even though quite painful. Then I got shingles and was cheerfully told by many that a trusted 'old wives' tale' had it that when the rash met round the middle you would die. It did not and I did not. This was followed by operations on both eyes - within a period of some six months - to remove cataracts. For ages the world seemed to be getting dimmer and the print in the altar missal less distinct, sign posts were mere splodges and the best way to drive was just to follow the car ahead and hope that he/she was going in my direction. The operations were very simple, I managed to drive on one eye at a time and not lift heavy weights for a few days, was continually being amazed at how bright colours could be but was bitterly disappointed with one aspect of life: not all the girls were beautiful.

The church heating packed up after a great flood filled the cellar (and, incidentally, drowned eleven tiny ducklings, all this during a Saturday evening Mass. I managed to bring the little bodies into the house in front of the gas fire and through warmth, warm milk and brandy, resurrected six of the bodies. They grew and matured, were tame and friendly only to be slaughtered by a fox all in one night some six months later). A new and very efficient system was eventually installed after some hand-to-hand fighting with the Diocesan financiers (whose delight it seems to be to complicate life for the simple) but the great, six foot deep hole in the middle of the aisle which used to blow out hot air was now a useless cavity. I suggested we ought to leave it there to serve as my grave eventually so that the parishioners could continue to walk all over me. Instead the incredible happened - the hole was filled in and a mosaic designed and laid by a Cranfield parishioner topped off the filling and nobody - absolutely nobody - criticised it, disliked the design, ever tripped over it or suggested we ought to have left the hole for posterity.

Time was passing, the old man getting older, changes constantly threatening, directives from the Diocese, from Health and Safety, Liturgical Commissions, Deanery initiatives, Ecumenical amalgamations, Musical and Catechetical innovations flooding in and getting more and more difficult to ignore as the parish did start getting into a comfortable and mostly (one hopes) happy rut. It seemed a good idea to tell the bishop about wanting to retire, set a date, prepare the parish by dishing out the multitude of little jobs the priest does simply because he is there and put into practice the long-held theory that an old priest in a parish starts doing more harm than good. After just over 18 years in Woburn Sands I retired, having served for close to 45 years all told, on January 1st 2004.

I am very grateful for surviving the war and then being accepted by this country and the Diocese. I feel I have been very fortunate in the parishes to which I had been sent and seemed to have been able to survive, even fall on my feet, throughout. I do not feel and do not even try to judge if and how much good effect I may have had through the years and with hindsight there are many things I would do very differently if there was a second time round, but I certainly do not regret having become a priest. In principle never ecstatically happy, I was more contented with my lot than I ever let on. But there is a deep sadness that through those years I seem to have 'presided' - no doubt with others - over a decline in faith and practice; and even a greater regret that we do not seem to have learnt very much.

We still worry about and even argue about so many things which are unimportant and have even been proved to have been negative and even harmful to people in general. But I retain a firm and simple belief that Our Lord, who founded the Church - people - knew and knows what he is doing, will continue to look after it in his own way and often probably in spite of all the brilliant ideas I myself and others have.

It would be fascinating to be around in the year 2225 or so to see just what a good job He will most certainly have done - and how the priesthood will have survived and changed: married priests, women priests, priests working with confidence doing the things for which ordination has marked them out, the people who make the Church playing a full part in the purpose for which the Church was founded.